The Neuroscience of Rhetoric in Management

Executives continue to lose their position because of inability to communicate organizational decisions to employees and boards effectively. More than just the words one writes or speaks, communication includes one's actions and other nonverbal attributes that carry meaning for audiences. Further, decisions may affect these audiences differently emotionally and economically, complicating communication with each group.

This book provides case studies to illustrate communication failure that directly resulted in executives' termination. These case studies include the fields of higher education, health care administration, computer technology, medical research, news media and advertising. Synthesizing scholarship in neuroscience about how the brain processes information from verbal, visual and other stimuli as well as management and communication principles found in books valued in leadership development programs, this book explains why audiences reacted negatively to messages and describes how the messages could have been delivered to get a better response. The book includes rubrics to assist readers to develop their own messages. Executives and those in leadership development programs will benefit from this book.

Dirk Remley is a Professor at Kent State University, USA.

T0384091

Routledge Focus on Business and Management

The fields of business and management have grown exponentially as areas of research and education. This growth presents challenges for readers trying to keep up with the latest important insights. Routledge Focus on Business and Management presents small books on big topics and how they intersect with the world of business research.

Individually, each title in the series provides coverage of a key academic topic, whilst collectively, the series forms a comprehensive collection across the business disciplines.

Stories for Management Success
The Power of Talk in Organizations
David Collins

How to Resolve Conflict in Organizations
The Power of People Models and Procedure
Annamaria Garden

Branding and Positioning in Base of Pyramid Markets in Africa
Innovative Approaches
Charles Blankson, Stanley Coffie and Joseph Darmoe

Persuasion
The Hidden Forces that Influence Negotiations
Jasper Kim

The Neuroscience of Rhetoric in Management
Compassionate Executive Communication
Dirk Remley

For more information about this series, please visit: www.routledge.com/ Routledge-Focus-on-Business-and-Management/book-series/FBM

The Neuroscience of Rhetoric in Management

Compassionate Executive Communication

Dirk Remley

Routledge
Taylor & Francis Group

NEW YORK AND LONDON

First published 2019
by Routledge
605 Third Avenue, New York, NY 10017

and by Routledge
2 Park Square, Milton Park, Abingdon, Oxon, OX14 4RN

First issued in paperback 2021

Routledge is an imprint of the Taylor & Francis Group, an informa business

Copyright © 2019 Taylor & Francis

Publisher's Note
The publisher has gone to great lengths to ensure the quality of this reprint
but points out that some imperfections in the original copies may be
apparent.

Library of Congress Cataloging-in-Publication Data
Names: Remley, Dirk, author.
Title: The neuroscience of rhetoric in management : compassionate
    executive communication / Dirk Remley.
Description: New York, NY : Routledge, 2019. | Series: Routledge focus
    on business and management | Includes bibliographical references
    and index.
Identifiers: LCCN 2018034615 | ISBN 9781138364813 (hardback) |
    ISBN 9780429431111 (ebook)
Subjects: LCSH: Communication in management. | Nonverbal
    communication in the workplace. | Leadership.
Classification: LCC HD57.7 .R46155 2019 | DDC 658.4/5—dc23
LC record available at https://lccn.loc.gov/2018034615

ISBN 13: 978-1-03-224180-7 (pbk)
ISBN 13: 978-1-138-36481-3 (hbk)

DOI: 10.4324/9780429431111

Typeset in Times New Roman
by Apex CoVantage, LLC

Contents

Figures

Prologue

Learning From Experience—Our Own and Others'

Leadership development occurs most productively through experiences. Articles and books can offer tips based on experiences, or research or even research based on experiences. Nevertheless, it is through experience that people learn valuable lessons connected to practices. If we have not yet experienced something, we listen to the stories of others who have experienced it. We learn from our own experiences as well as from others' experiences.

This book offers consideration of several experiences others had toward helping the reader learn to communicate well in leadership positions. For the most part, I focus on executive-level communication—communication associated with the highest levels of an organization. However, these stories can be applied at almost any level in which one assumes a leadership role.

One reads periodically about a CEO who was forced to resign or who was fired because of a communication-related snafu. The incident, or series of incidents, occurs in spite of the executive's prior experiences and own professional development related to leadership. Why? Part of the answer is because executives deal with many audiences and are trying to make everyone happy, or they are trying to please one they feel is most important. Sometimes these audiences compete with each other. Not enough books deal with this competition.

I offer two examples of this competition within my own experiences in leadership positions here to illustrate a couple of points. The cases I provide in the book may offer examples with which readers who have high-level aspirations can relate; however, these two examples are relevant for many reasons.

I have never been an executive at a Fortune 500 company, guiding it through difficult financial times. I have never led a military task force into what many considered a suicide mission, completing the mission successfully and returning all without a scratch. I have never led a rag-tag team of misfits that lost almost all of its games in one season to a championship in the next season. Nevertheless, I have experienced some dynamics of executive/

leadership-related communication from which I have learned, and others can learn. They suggest that leadership communication often involves experimentation, and it involves trying to meet the needs of multiple audiences.

Case 1

I participated in my institution's leadership development program. The program included a few elements typical of such programs, including some self-tests related to leadership qualities, experiences, feedback from others ("360-degree feedback") and emotional intelligence testing. It, also, required participants to create and act on a leadership project in which we would receive feedback pre- and post-experience, having implemented certain leadership qualities based on that 360-degree assessment.

Background

My career field (rhetoric and composition/writing studies) is generally recognized as female-dominated; that is, there are more females in the field than males. One needs only to attend national conferences to see this representation as well. My activity in this field tends to focus on forms of workplace writing and communication, such as business writing, technical writing and professional writing. I have been involved in teaching such courses, developing such courses and mentoring graduate students in scholarship and teaching of such courses. My research has, also, revolved around issues and theories related to it, much like this book.

At the time that I was enrolled in the program, my institution was implementing a new business writing course, that I was to coordinate, while redesigning an old course—business and professional writing—that had been used for the purpose of the new course. The old course had been required of all business majors, and it was open to other major programs as well. The new course would be open only to business majors, while the old course would be open to other majors; however, the old course needed to be redesigned so as not to overlap in content with the new course. The task that I chose for my leadership project involved creating a mentoring program for graduate students who would be teaching the new course. However, I, also, was involved on the committee to redesign the old course. One of the members of this committee was among those providing feedback on my 360-degree assessment.

Attributes of Focus

On the pre-activity assessment, I received feedback indicating relatively low scores for being assertive and presenting ideas that may not be popular.

While I am a male, I tend to try to be respectful of others' perspectives and exercise empathy. This was evidenced in my results for the emotional intelligence testing. The director of the program, in reviewing my scores with me, acknowledged that mine were among the highest scores they had experienced in the program. Another member of my cohort, in fact, had similarly high scores.

Because we had to identify traits from the 360-degree assessment to work on toward improving, I decided I would work on those two items: being more assertive and presenting ideas that may not be popular. So, the feedback tells a heterosexual male to be more assertive and raise points that may not be popular. I would be doing this in a setting that included an audience of only women.

As I made this decision and conveyed it within my leadership cohort, I acknowledged concern about being perceived as a jerk. I was reassured by the person directing the program (a male) that this perception would not be likely to happen, as the people involved had a history with me and knew of my general demeanor. So, I moved forward with my effort. I would try to be more assertive while still trying to be respectful of others. I would not seek out opportunities to be assertive or raise points that may not be popular; however, I would not hesitate to act on them if the opportunity presented itself. Further, someone else involved in the 360-degree assessment—my immediate supervisor (a female)—was aware of what I was doing.

Implementation and Observation

Such opportunities presented themselves a few times during the course of our work in the committee. However, these tended to be in the form of reminding those on the committee of some caveats that I was told (by a female colleague who was also on this committee) as I developed the new course regarding potential content overlap with existing courses. The administration did not want much overlap in content between two or more courses, which makes sense; why offer two courses that do pretty much the same content? Nevertheless, these seemed to come across as statements that slowed the committees' work down.

I mention gender of some people involved in this case, because it may have affected perception of some of my actions; I describe this point in another chapter; however, there are gender differences that affect leadership communication attributes. That information also helps to explain the next paragraph here.

I sensed some animosity about my statements, and I discussed this with my supervisor. I, also, discussed the concern within my cohort. As the second round of 360-degree assessments occurred (post-activity), we found that there was considerable backlash regarding my new approach. The one person on the committee even wrote that I seemed to have "an agenda" within the committee; and someone else, with whom that person spoke regularly, indicated that I worked well by myself but not with others. My supervisor indicated that I was trying to work with a "tough group" and that I should try to be more of "the knowledgeable colleague."

That last statement is important relative to gender-leadership communication style elements discussed further in the book.

Case 2

At about the same time as I experienced the leadership development program, I was appointed to the position of course coordinator for a business writing course that would be required of all business majors at my institution. In this position, I would find myself trying to balance the needs and practices of two very different audiences. This caused considerable consternation and stress for me, ending with a financial decision to no longer require the course.

Background

The College of Business (CoB) at my institution wanted to develop a new business writing course that had a closer focus to its needs. The existing course had been offered through the Department of English, and CoB was concerned about some approaches to the course that were influenced by trends in writing studies instruction best practices. Through a series of events, they were able to develop a newer course with a focus on their students' needs. Further, they would have considerable input in developing the course content.

They approached me to lead development of the course and to coordinate the implementation of it. Implementation included standardization of pedagogy across sections to ensure that all students had the same learning experience and exposure to the same material. This would facilitate assessment of their learning better than if each instructor had a large degree of autonomy. Several sections of the course would eventually be offered, requiring that a number of other instructors learn how the course should be taught. So, as coordinator, it would be my job to mentor these teachers and make sure they taught as CoB needed the course to be taught. Most of these instructors would be female.

This was okay with me, because standardization of teaching had been increasing nationally; though, scholarship in writing studies teaching encouraged some autonomy so instructors could address the needs of individual students better. I acknowledged this approach to CoB's administration, and they conveyed approval for some degree of autonomy within a generally standardized course. That is, all sections would include the exact same content, assignments/activities, but individual instructors could include their own exercises beyond the common ones as needed. All started out well. I was able to balance the CoB's position of standardized pedagogy with "best practices" valued in writing studies and with which those I led were accustomed.

Growing Pains

As the number of sections increased, more teachers became involved. I continued with the program of facilitating some autonomy while maintaining standardized pedagogy. However, I found the CoB administration increasingly wanting more standardization across sections. I continued to negotiate for some degree of autonomy, but this was reduced to only one activity. I had crossed one "line in the sand" between what CoB valued and what general scholarship in writing studies valued. More of the course would be consistent across sections. Because it was a service course—a course that serves the needs of another program, outside of the Department of English—I tried to work with the CoB's administration while allowing for the autonomy valued in writing studies scholarship. Stress levels increased as this occurred.

The following academic year, CoB would raise concerns that some instructors were teaching content they did not value—essays. Essays are the primary form of academic writing, and CoB wanted to avoid essays in the class. Generally, essays are not a part of business writing courses, and I understood that and had discouraged essays. When I asked the teachers if any were having students write essays, all denied it. I was challenged to defend the teachers I led.

Defending them was not difficult, but getting CoB to understand was. At one meeting with CoB, the administrator acknowledged that a member of a student advisory board explained that they had an essay in which they had to write a memo responding to a given scenario. A memo is a recognized business writing genre, yet the student labeled it as an essay. It was evident that the student had defaulted to referring to any piece of assigned writing as an essay, and CoB did not challenge the student's perception. This was a second "line in the sand" I had to address.

Consequently, in spite of my clarifying the situation and defending the teachers, CoB never believed that students were not being asked to write essays. I had come up against two competing ideologies, and I was losing trust from the audience that "controlled" the course's relevance.

Eventually (year 4 of the program), CoB's administration demanded that I standardize everything about the course. This was a third "line in the sand." It seemed as if they wanted me to provide the instructors a script to facilitate teaching, while no one would have any degree of autonomy. This did not go over well with the instructors. Some snuck their own activities into their section of the course while maintaining most of the standardized approach. Nevertheless, CoB conveyed dissatisfaction. It rose to a point where I felt that I would need to create a script not only for the instructors but also for the students so they understood what terminology to use.

Subsequently, the administration in the CoB found a way to eliminate the course as a requirement and move the writing "instruction" entirely online and into one of their existing management courses. Because of the budget model at my institution, this would also generate more revenue for the CoB, something it had been trying to accomplish with its initial effort to gain control of the course.

Lesson

Again, I was dealing with two very different audiences (three if we consider the students' propensity to call assigned writing "essays."). I was dealing with the administration of the CoB, which valued complete standardization; and I was dealing with instructors who had learned to value autonomy while meeting course learning objectives.

In many meetings with CoB, I argued for some level of autonomy while trying to meet their needs; however, they became less willing to negotiate that autonomy. In many meetings with the instructors, I explained that I did not value complete standardization but it was something CoB "needed" of us. I did this to try to help them understand why we had such standardization.

At some point, the balancing act had to fall apart because of the competing values between the two audiences. It is a challenge to appeal to such diverse audiences. Further, CoB was asking me to use a management style I did not value—imposing its will (through me) on my "team." I was in a position in which I had to make decisions on actions that I did not necessarily support, yet I tried to communicate with each audience to help it understand how best to teach the course. While my values lined up with those of the team I led, it was contrary to what the CoB wanted. While I understood CoB's "needs," the team did not value that approach, and members resisted.

The two stories here illustrate a few points that I detail in the chapters of this book: The challenges executives have to face from dealing with multiple audiences from different perspectives, and the need to be able to manage both audiences through communication.

1 Introduction

The Role of Communication in Managing People

Many publications identify organizational skill, decision-making, creating a vision or objective, coordinating work of a team and motivating people among the top leadership and management skills required for the position. Recently, Fernandez-Araoz et al. (2017) cited these skills as competencies required to be a great leader. Inherent in all of these skills is communication. However, communication is many things.

The words one uses are the most obvious form of communication. However, nonverbal elements such as one's appearance, the way one looks at others and their actions generally, also, carry a message. Each of these is a mode of representation; that is, a way of representing a message to others visually, orally, spatially and with words—print-linguistic text—among other modes of representation. When these forms of representation are combined, they form a multimodal message. When I speak with someone face-to-face, she experiences a multimodal message:

1. She sees my facial expressions and general appearance (visual/nonverbal). My expression may suggest concern, surprise or satisfaction; and my general appearance, including my dress, may suggest professionalism or comfort (visual/nonverbal);
2. She hears my words (oral/aural), which may be at a certain volume to represent normal tone or louder to suggest emphasis;
3. I might stand a certain distance from her (spatial) either to respect her space or to suggest authority over her, and
4. I might shake her hand or tap her on the arm (touch/haptic) as I make a point to try to convey importance of the point or represent a collegial bond with her.

As suggested with the description related to each mode, the combination of the modes influences the specific message conveyed holistically. My dress may reinforce the formal tone of my words to suggest professionalism. I can reinforce professional respect by smiling courteously as I use formal language. Much communication is multimodal, limited only by the media involved or physical presence. Is one communicating face-to-face with their audience? Is one e-mailing a message? Talking over the phone? Video conferencing? Writing a report to be attached to an e-mail message or mailed? Each of these contexts facilitates certain modalities, emphasizing a limited set while possibly excluding others.

Managers and executives can communicate using any of these methods—email, phone, face-to-face, video conferencing or document reporting. Managers and executives, also, communicate through actions. Even when not directly communicating with someone, actions convey messages visually and spatially that a given audience may perceive certain ways. If one donates money to a cause within a workplace fundraising effort, the action is perceived as supporting that effort—supporting the organization. If one closes his office door, it suggests that he does not want to see others.

Also, the kinds of messages managers and executives must make tend to involve a certain range that are typically associated with elements of leadership: Inspiring people to act on decisions, articulating a vision for the organization, building trust, facilitating change, conveying responsibility and knowledge while being a team player.

However, how does one communicate these elements? Further, rarely is a message a single interaction. A single message, indeed, may be part of a larger series of messages an audience absorbs related to a given activity. What is the relationship among these messages?

Books and articles about management and leadership are loaded with principles and tips associated with the various elements involved in leadership and management, like those identified above. Some present examples of successful managers to illustrate application of those concepts. The value in using such examples is that they act as case studies that readers may be able to emulate. A reader may imitate people in those cases and become successful. However, much as it is important to understand successful examples of leadership, it is important to understand what contributes to failed leadership. One can learn more from failure than from success.

A growing number of recent works describe the use of empathy, or "emotional intelligence," in decision-making and communication. Broadly, the concept describes the use of an understanding of others' feelings in making decisions and communicating those decisions. The gist is that doing so will help the audience respond favorably to the decision. However, this concept becomes difficult to apply as the size of an audience grows. Managers may be dealing with a team of 4–10 people or more. Executives deal with many teams of varying sizes. Also, an interesting attribute of executive communication is that some of it may become public.

I detail applications of emotional intelligence and a couple of other related concepts in this book. Further, I use concepts of neuroscience to explain why principles associated with these concepts tend to work well. In addition to the social dynamics involved in communication, there are biological phenomena that are affected by social interactions over time. An understanding of these phenomena can help one plan future interactions.

Purpose of Book

With this book I attempt to provide managers and executives with an understanding of how to communicate the kinds of messages related to leadership in the various modes identified in the first paragraphs, among various audiences/teams and integrating elements of emotional intelligence and neuroscience. Such a book is not new to the field.

There are three things that make this book different from those sources:

1. I temper the treatment of the executive relative to employees/subordinates with consideration of pressures the executive experiences from others— the board of directors, for example—to show how one may balance potentially competing audiences; and
2. I use specific examples of failure to illustrate consequences of not communicating effectively while, also, offering alternate messages to address the situation in a better way.
3. I clarify the perception of emotional intelligence with Bloom's (2016) the concept of "rational compassion."

Board Versus Employees

In leadership studies, the focus tends to be on how to manage others who are subordinates or part of a team of employees, including communicating with them. There is less information about how to balance communication with those employees and with the people who manage the executive—the board of directors, trustees, those who may be the only one to whom an executive reports. While articles about how to communicate with boards exist, they tend to focus on just the board as an audience, not considering the implications of employee audiences.

Each of the case studies I present includes consideration of both sets of audiences: the leadership team (executive and board or "superior") and the employees (or "subordinates"). While everyone involved in an organization wants the organization to succeed, different audiences have different sets of concerns that affect their perception of how to address organizational challenges. These are impacted by various elements that can be embedded in the biology of the brain—neuroscientific makeup. So, I include the connections to neuroscience as I discuss how each audience may respond to a given message.

The Value of Failure

Instead of presenting information generally about such messages, as is typically the case in such books, I provide concrete examples that readers can use in various situations. As such, this book provides a practical toolkit that one can use to build a rationally compassionate message.

I use a few examples of success; however, as indicated, I draw on concrete examples of leadership failure to illustrate the value of communication within leadership. In each of the cases I present, there is a disconnect associated with communication from the executive to others, as reported in media outlets. One case is particularly interesting to me, because the person involved identified a certain leadership-related, best-selling book as a favored and influential book for them when they were hired into the executive position that I use as a case study of failure.

The book, *Good to Great*, by Jim Collins, was published in 2001. In it, Collins offers a number of examples of successful leadership relative to his theory of the Level 5 leader (more on this later). However, there is some debate about the value of the examples. Levitt (2008) criticized it as limited in its examination of historical successes and not able to offer much help for future application; nevertheless, it is generally through historical examination of cases that we learn. Indeed, Murray (2010) identified it among the best management books based on feedback from the Wall Street Journal's CEO Council. Finally, it is used in many leadership development programs, including the one that I experienced in 2015—a program that LEAD ranked highly among education-related certificate programs in leadership/organizational development in 2018 (HR.com, 2018).

I formulate a means to apply elements of that book with two other books identified in management circles as influential: *The Emotionally Intelligent Manager*, by David Caruso and Peter Salovey; and *Emotional Intelligence 2.0*, by Travis Bradberry and Jeanne Greaves. However, there seems to be some misunderstanding associated with the application of empathy presented in these books.

Rational Compassion and Emotional Intelligence

Generally, emotional intelligence involves understanding one's own emotions, understanding others' emotions, understanding how to manage them and how to use them in communicating with others. *The Emotionally Intelligent*

Manager was published in 2004. It was used in the leadership development program that I experienced in 2015, and Jenson (2017) lists it among the best workplace-related books about emotional intelligence currently. According to Mulvey (2017), *Emotional Intelligence 2.0* is among Amazon.com's best-selling books on management and leadership. It is safe to say that these 3 books have been used in leadership/executive development by many people, even if in informal training.

Many seem to perceive these books to encourage empathy in dealing with others. However, this is a misperception. Authors of both books qualify how to apply empathy, though this qualification is treated minimally. Bloom (2016) calls attention to the hazard of too much empathy, and he seems to help clarify what the other books suggest about applying empathy to decisions.

Bloom (2016) explains that applying empathy to decision-making and messages generally becomes counterproductive. Bloom suggests an over-emphasis on empathy, or effort to be empathetic, in work on social psychology generally. He argues that one can feel sorry for another and consider others' feelings without becoming overly sensitive to those feelings. Over-sensitivity to others' feelings can lead to a bad decision. Bloom states that empathy is "different from being compassionate, from being kind, and most of all, from being good" (p. 4). He suggests that empathy "has been oversold" (p. 7). Further, he argues that this focus on empathy and effort to empathize with others is "myopic" and leads to poor decisions with long-term implications (p. 31).

Executives address several audiences and may have to convey messages that some people will not like. Even with an audience of one, that one person may disagree with a decision that benefits an organization. So, it is unreasonable to expect an executive to be able to implement a decision that acts on empathy with all audiences, or all members of a single audience.

However, even the literature about emotional intelligence qualifies that one can be compassionate while making a decision that is not popular (Caruso and Salovey, 2004 and Bradberry and Greaves, 2009). Some seem to perceive that emotional intelligence equates to emphasis on empathy, and these books can present a confusing representation of the application of empathy in decisions and messages. Leadership coach Cindy Wigglesworth (2013) explains that compassion suggests a degree of empathy, but it does not commit to acting on that empathy. It is much easier to act on and convey compassion than to express empathy through action. So, I emphasize the term "compassionate intelligence" here.

"Compassionate intelligence" clarifies "emotional intelligence." It is the ability to: understand other perspectives, use those perspectives in a rational decision that benefits the organization, and communicate that consideration such that the audience is aware of the balance between their perspective(s) and emotional needs and the organization's needs.

Background Basics

I present the principles associated with these books here, showing interconnections among them and some neuroscientific concepts that are also relevant such as mirror neurons and reward neurons. Later, I relate them, especially, to those leadership attributes identified in the first paragraph of this chapter toward synthesizing particular elements of multimodal messages within leadership contexts. This enables me to provide the basic theory framing the analyses in the rest of the book to show applications.

Good to Great

Collins (2001) starts by presenting a hierarchy of skills and attributes associated with leadership, which he calls the "Level 5 Hierarchy" (p. 20). Collins represents the hierarchy as a pyramid, with Level 1 at the bottom and Level 5 at the top. He notes that the pyramid/hierarchy is not necessarily a stepladder, in which each rung is separate from the others below it. Each level includes the attributes of the level(s) below it and adds another trait. The Level 5 executive integrates all the attributes associated with the other 4 levels (p. 21).

In Figure 1.1 I summarize Collins' description of each level (column on the left), and I add some characterization of communication skills related to each (column on the right).

The majority of Collins' book presents case studies in which he applies another theoretical construct—the "Black Box" in which exists a "flywheel" and process that facilitates advancing a company from getting good results to getting great results. This Black Box and process start with the Level 5 Leader and involve their ability to develop a strong team and to communicate various messages associated with leadership: vision, discipline, change (potentially), innovation while using various resources.

Relevance to Theory—Defining Team(s)

An observation from the case studies that I present later regarding executive failure and related to Collins' text is that their failure was not so much related to the "Black Box" Collins details or with lack of skill at a given level of the Level 5 pyramid. The failure was in communicating with the different audiences with which the executive works relative to a given level and audience. Executives are members of multiple teams and managing them may become difficult.

Level and Collins' Characterization	Related Communication Skills
1: Those who make good contributions because of their knowledge, skill and work habits.	Involves basic skills associated with business communication—clarity and conciseness.
2: Applying those Level 1 attributes in a team environment, working well with others while contributing their personal traits and skills to attain the team's objectives.	The ability to communicate respect for others in a team environment as well as make compromises and listen carefully to others' concerns and ideas. These build trust.
3: Brings the general leadership principle of organizational skill to the mix with the team concept conveyed in Level 2. The person not only contributes to the team, but facilitates coordination and organization of teamwork	Some advanced competence with communication skills toward being able to communicate responsibilities and organization to others while persuading toward attaining goal/task. Also, conveying support for others and offering productive feedback. The latter two contribute to trust-building.
4: Shows commitment to organization's vision while motivating others toward excellence. As such, they are taking on more attributes of a leadership role.	Ability to motivate and convey a broader organizational goal toward persuading others to buy into the goals and perform beyond acceptable standard. Also, express ways to accomplish vision and ways leadership will support others. The latter two help maintain trust.
5: The ability to sustain organizational success through one's personal traits, balancing humility with commitment	This involves the ability to communicate change decisions to help the organization continue its successes or adapt to the environment while emphasizing others' role in that continued success. Express how leadership will facilitate transition.

Figure 1.1 "Level 5 Hierarchy" and Communication

Executives may have two very different audiences they are trying to please. Of course, we always perceive the main audience of the leader as her underlings—the employees, from those immediately below her in the company's hierarchy to the bottom level. Even at the middle management level, leadership communication generally focuses on communication with underlings. However, there is another audience for the executive: the board of directors or trustees . . . whoever hired that executive or ranks above her in the organization's hierarchy.

Relative to the concept of working within a team, the leader becomes a member of two teams: 1) the executive team—president and VPs as well as executive board members, and 2) the managers and employees under him. There is a certain mirroring of each other within a team environment; at the most basic level, we mirror each other's values with regard, especially, to attaining the objective of the team. Even as we have different skill sets, we embrace our likeness with regard to having that common value. This can become a challenge when we are on multiple teams at once. The leader needs to be able to communicate with both sets of team members effectively.

The executive is trying to meet the needs of two potentially different audiences. The board of directors may be concerned with (value) the bottom line, while workers are concerned about (value) their employment and any input they may have in decisions. When there is a disconnect associated with the messages connected to these audiences and their values, one side will react negatively even as the other reacts positively. The executive board will react positively to the message of change being proposed to "right" the organization toward profitability; the employee may react with fear that she will lose her job, or her job will become more challenging as she has to learn a new way of doing it.

The theory—and practice—must integrate that consideration: managing multiple audiences associated with a given message.

The Emotionally Intelligent Manager

At the very basis of Caruso and Salovey's text is the notion that emotions: cannot be ignored, affect decisions and should be integrated into decision-making (pp. 9–21). Because of this, managers need to learn how to understand how to use emotion effectively—their own as well as those of others with whom they work.

They move from that foundation to a process associated with using this understanding of emotions and how to manage it:

1. Understand the situation, including the people involved
2. Identify feelings of those involved
3. Describe the focus of attention
4. Understand emotions: why do people feel a certain way about the focus of attention
5. Manage feelings of those involved

(p. 25)

The rest of Caruso and Salovey's book describes ways to understand people's emotions, including one's own, and how to use and manage them.

This includes application of what Bloom (2016) calls "rational compassion." However, these concepts and their application can be confusing. Caruso and Salovey seem to offer coaching to help one recall specific feelings associated with certain emotions. This coaching includes experiencing specific biological attributes: breathing, heart rate, location of discomfort (stomach, chest, . . .). They encourage the reader to feel all the feelings (emotional and physical) associated with certain emotions, including fear, anger and happiness among others (pp. 109–111). They provide a hypothetical case when a manager applied too much rationalization to avoid potential risk (pp. 189–192). However, in the same vicinity of the book, they also point out that it may be problematic to make a decision based on what the audience wants instead of what the leader believes is appropriate, especially when there may be too much emotion driving a group's perceptions (pp. 186–188).

The caveat is that, while one should try to understand emotions of all involved, one must not become irrational while trying to be empathetic by ignoring what he understands to be needed for the company's best interest. It is dangerous to over-emphasize empathy/emotions and ignore rationality.

Relevance to Theory—Sensitivity

As suggested earlier, everyone involved in the effect of a decision experiences some kind of emotions. They may be happy about the decision, they may be sad, they may be frustrated, they may be afraid. The more one who makes these decisions and communicates them understands these emotions, the better one may be at addressing or managing them within a message. Further, one needs to consider their own emotional reaction to a given decision, especially if there is a conflict with values.

The effective manager mirrors the values of his employees as well as his superiors. When making decisions, one needs to mirror the decision-making process valued by those on that team. In multiple cases that I present later, the leader failed to mirror the values of an audience, and this disconnect became evident within forms of communication with the audiences. However, evidence of a possible communication problem related to this sensitivity to others existed before they were hired into the particular executive position.

Theory—and practice—reflect this need to mirror the team's values and communicating them, which can be done using various methods.

Emotional Intelligence 2.0

Expanding on the concepts presented by Caruso and Salovey, Bradberry and Greaves offer a few additional details and tips about developing an understanding of the roles emotions play, how to understand them in oneself as well as in others, and provide some tests to assess one's own ability to do so. They, also, provide some conceptualization of relationship-building (Chapter 8). Relationship-building tips include:

1. Enhance your own communication style, including the ability to adjust
2. Avoid giving mixed signals
3. Remember the little things that work
4. Accept feedback graciously
5. Build trust, including "consistency in words, action, behaviors over time" (p. 191)
6. Use anger purposefully
7. Acknowledge others' emotions
8. Explain decisions (p. 179)

This list is not comprehensive in terms of what they list about relationship-building; in fact, they list 17 items. However, the items I list pertain directly to communication elements I found in the cases I include later.

I call attention, especially, to items 2 and 5 in my list above—avoiding mixed signals and building trust through words, actions and behaviors. This echoes the statement in the first paragraph of this book—that one communicates not only with words but through actions and behaviors. One may recall the adage that "actions speak louder than words." If our actions are contrary to our words—whether because of action or inaction—people will quickly lose trust in us. Our words and actions must mirror the values of the team(s) of which we are a member.

I, also, note items 7 and 8; these two recognize that, even when making decisions with which others will not agree, one can still exercise some degree of empathy, or compassion, by acknowledging others' emotions and explaining why a given decision is the right one. The acknowledgment of others' emotions gives credibility to their consideration, and the explanation can link the decision explicitly to the needs of the organization. Bradberry and Greaves also explain the benefit of acknowledging others' feelings (p. 201) and explaining decisions that may upset people (pp. 208–209) when communicating decisions that will not be popular.

Relevance to Theory—Trust Through Empathy

Mirror neurons process what we see and perceive in others' actions relative to what we understand of them and how we interpret the world. They contribute to cognition in helping us draw conclusions about those observations.

Theory—and practice—need to include consideration of consistency of words and behaviors.

If we see someone behaving in a way we value or that reflects an understanding of our own position, it is perceived favorably. If their words are consistent with that behavior, our favorable perception of the person is reinforced. If, however, their behaviors do not reflect their words, we begin to distrust our perception of them.

Studies have found that trust is, perhaps, the most important attribute in persuasion. If an audience believes in what the speaker/communicator is saying, they will follow. If they do not trust the speaker, they will not likely follow or will hesitate and follow cautiously, slowing down potential progress. As soon as an audience loses trust in someone (or never had trust in them, for whatever reason), the relationship between leader and audience is damaged, negatively affecting other elements of leadership.

The Role of Neuroscience in Emotional Intelligence

As I mentioned before, mirror neurons facilitate much of the cognition associated with watching someone do something and in doing it yourself. Mirror neurons are active as one observes activity that one wants to emulate or with which one wants to assimilate. Mirror neurons are involved in persuasion. An audience wants to mirror some aspect of the speaker, or the speaker may want to reflect some quality of the audience to assimilate with it more.

I have mentioned in previous work that mirror neurons behave differently in persuasive exchanges than they do in instructional exchanges. While they facilitate imitation within instructional contexts, they help facilitate a shared experience between speaker and audience in persuasive contexts (Remley, 2017). This represents a different relationship between communicator and audience relative to context: instructional versus persuasive. Trust is part of persuasion.

I have, also, written about the role of "reward neurons" in persuasion. If one is made aware of a particular reward associated with doing something, and she values that reward, she is more motivated to attain that reward. If the value of a given reward is shared between the manager and the audience, that value is mirrored; there may be overlap between the impact of mirror neurons and reward neurons.

Between these two kinds of neurons and the scholarship on emotional intelligence there is a common thread: People like to know that they share common values with others they look up to or follow and are respected by these others. The principles of emotional intelligence identified above focus on explicitly making connections with others' emotions—understanding their fears/concerns/values and balancing the needs of the task with their emotional needs.

The teacher who uses instructional materials that connect to students' values and help the students understand certain concepts through valued reward systems and cognitive styles will be able to help the students learn better than the teacher who does not. The manager who helps his team members understand their roles within the team effort, support their work and motivate them through rewards they value will be able to get the team to accomplish the task. The executive who balances the needs of the organization with the emotional needs of his employees ensures the organization's success. The executive, manager or teacher who cannot meet these needs is doomed to fail.

The executive who is able to successfully balance the needs of the organization with the needs of her employees is able to gain and maintain employees' and the board's trust. As soon as trust is damaged, failure is likely. A fascinating phenomenon related to the neuroscience of each of these audiences—boards and employees—needs to be understood and, often, is not. I hope to address that lack of understanding with this book.

The Dangers of Empathy in Decision-Making

A lot of publications present how important empathy is in team leadership. I have identified only a few in the first chapter. The dangers associated with engaging empathy in a workplace environment are valid concerns; so, I recognize them and address them.

Again, Caruso & Salovey and Bradberry & Greaves separately acknowledge the need to exercise empathy with caution, especially with difficult situations and messages. Bloom (2016) covers a range of interactions related to morality (distinguishing right from wrong), not just within business settings. He identifies three particular issues with empathy that may be related to business contexts:

1.   It can become a heavy emotional weight to bear.
2.   It can make one numb to others.
3.   It may negatively affect judgment.

Bloom, a social psychologist who has published on child development and morality, defines "empathy" in a traditional sense of the word—feeling what others feel—while suggesting other connotations (p. 40). If one empathizes with others, he or she is able to experience emotionally the same feelings that other person feels. This may cause the person empathizing with the other not to make good decisions affecting himself or those around him. Bloom states that empathy is myopic in that it flashes a spotlight on the one with whom we empathize. That one person's, or group's, feelings are emphasized over all others.

Bloom goes on to distinguish this from feeling sorry for someone—sympathy/compassion, which he considers a more appropriate response to others' emotions and more realistic. It is possible to care about others through compassion while making rational decisions, but compassion is different from empathy.

Emotional Intelligence Caveats

Applying Bloom's consideration to emotional intelligence, the articles and books that encourage development of emotional intelligence talk about listening to others toward understanding their feelings. An executive may need to listen to scores of stories and reactions to situations. The more one hears of anxieties, concerns and negative experiences of others, the more of an emotional toll it takes on the listener. Each person has his or her own story and response to it. The sum of these experiences may seem like a huge hurdle to overcome. However, one needs to manage the information, like a computer program manages data gathered toward producing findings about it.

As one accumulates these stories, rather than becoming more sensitive to others' emotions, one becomes numb. Like seeing hundreds of soldiers killed on a battlefield in wartime, while traumatic emotionally at first, one has to find a way to manage it; one way is to perceive that it is part of the context and move forward. At a certain point, rather than listen to another story, one stops listening as the other person speaks, numb to the nature of the story generally.

Finally, as one becomes numb to the emotions of others within a given context, one no longer makes decisions based on emotional effect. It seems like the person no longer cares about others, and he acts like a machine. In a couple of the cases presented later in this book, it will become evident that the executive is making decisions exclusively based on financial data rather than including the relevant emotional data in the decision process.

Considering these problems, Bloom encourages compassion while being rational. In the end, the bottom line may be the financials reporting all the results of various decisions one makes; however, the emotional impact of those decisions can have a large impact on people who contribute to them. So, decision processes need to include consideration of others' emotions; however, they should not depend entirely on them. Clarke (2018) states, "While empathy can certainly be used to inform decisions within appropriate contexts, leaders benefit most by taking a considerate and thoughtful approach to their decision-making" (paragraph 44). Nevertheless, one can convey the valuation of others' perspectives and emotions within a decision process. This may act to represent some degree of empathy while having to meet the needs of the entire organization.

Synthesizing these principles, a theory of a "compassionately intelligent executive" emerges to inform executive communication. This theory combines Collins' principles of the Level 5 Hierarchy, emotional intelligence, and rational compassion and neuroscientific principles inherent in each.

Perspectives

The first concept is perspective and how one needs to consider how their message may be interpreted by others. Others are likely to apply their own prior experiences, values and perceptions of the speaker's trustworthiness to an interpretation. So, the message needs to integrate explicit cues for the audience to interpret the message a certain way—the way you want them to interpret it so as to come across as compassionate. That is, your message (be it just words, or a combination of words, visuals and actions) exposes several attributes of itself and the speaker/writer to the audience. These attributes are relative to the audience's perception, though, not your own.

A short set of executive communication attributes emerges from the synthesis of these works. While expressing him or herself and his or her own ideas, the executive needs to convey respect for others as well as support of their work and concerns. Such respect and support are demonstrated various ways: explicit invitation to contribute, expressions of appreciation for their ideas/concerns, openness to their ideas. The message needs to show recognition of others' ideas and feelings while expressing hope and ways leadership will support them through their labor and/or any change. Engaging others' previous experiences, especially successes, as well as indicating how they will benefit from implementation of executive decisions will help to facilitate acceptance of those decisions.

The rubric in Figure 1.2 represents the various attributes that affect an audience's perception of a message and a means by which one can design a message effectively applying the several concepts presented in this chapter.

Later, I provide a rubric that includes example messages relative to their effectiveness and the criteria in this rubric.

While suggesting just words, a rubric representing multimodal messages emerges further:

As one reads this book, it is important to understand how to use the information. The lesson here is not that one should listen to his or her employees, synthesize their emotions and make decisions with which all will be happy. The lesson is that one should listen to employees and board members to understand their feelings and concerns toward understanding what decision to make that they will be able to accept *and toward understanding how to phrase that message.*

COMPASSIONATE INTELLIGENCE LEVEL	PERSPECTIVE	PRIOR EXPERIENCE	MIRROR NEURON ACTIVATION	REWARD NEURON ACTIVATION	TRUST-BUILDING
Superior	Very sensitive to others' views; explicit acknowledgement of consideration; acknowledgement of various perspectives involved. Reference to some statements of others	High consideration of others' experiences and recognizes value; reference to others' statements	High explicit recognition of values of all audiences involved experiences	Explicit acknowledgement of potential, specific reward valued by all audiences involved	Makes explicit connection between own experiences/ values and those of audience
Good	Somewhat sensitive to others' views; acknowledges others' input; summarizes some statements of others	Some consideration of others' experiences and implicit recognition of value; summarizing experiences	Reference to recognition of values in experiences	Explicit acknowledgement of potential reward valued by audience	Suggests connection between own experiences/values and those of all audiences involved
Reasonable	Suggests sensitivity to others' views by acknowledging others' input and consideration in decision process. Mentions types of narratives involved	Suggests consideration of others' experiences and implicit recognition of value in decision process. Mentions one experience	Reference to recognition of values in experiences	acknowledgement of potential, generalized reward valued by audience	Suggests connection between own experiences/ values and an audience involved
Need to improve	Mentions others' input	No mention of consideration of others' experiences in decision	Generalized statement of something valued by audiences	Generalized statement of potential rewards	Little suggestion of shared experience/ values with audience.

Figure 1.2 Compassionate Executive Communication Rubric

Mode	Visual (what audience sees)	Aural (what audience hears)	Spatial (positioning relative to audience(s)	Appearance (what person looks like)
Superior	Inviting demeanor; open door policy; near employees; interacts periodically and regularly	Pleasant; Encouraging; positive tone	Comfortable Respectful near employees interacts periodically and regularly	Professional not too much better than others
Good	Inviting, open door policy	Pleasant Open, positive tone	Respectful, open to employees	Professional, a bit 'above' that of employees
Borderline Reasonable	Inviting official	Official Professional neutral tone	Official distance, may seem intimidating, respectful	Very official. much higher than others' 'position'
Needs Work	Intimidating	Official Angry disappointed	Hovers or too distant inaccessible	Very dressy professional while employees wear blue collar wear.

Figure 1.2 (Continued)

It is impossible to make everyone happy about some decisions that need to be acted upon. Change is very stressful, and many do not want to have to change their routine. Nevertheless, change may be what an organization needs to survive. Emotional intelligence and empathy can inform the ways change occurs and how change is presented to employees.

The book is concise for a reason: its emphasis is on practice. I refer to a number of sources of information to help the reader understand principles and their value. An assumption I make about the reader, because the targeted audience is professionals—managers and executives as well as those in executive development programs—is that the reader already has some understanding of basic elements of communication. This may be from their educational background, professional development and/or experiences. The reader does not need a review of those basics.

Each chapter starts with a short section providing some background related to the chapter's topic. This is, generally, not more than one page. The remainder of the chapter includes practical tips and examples to address the specific kind of message related to the chapter. As such, the hope is that one can keep this book near their desk as a quick reference tool or guide.

Case Study Methodology

While theory is of value in developing a framework to understand and conceptualize the world around us, specific events and experiences shape theory. Specific experiences, also, help to understand why a theory may not have worked. The narrative of experience becomes more meaningful than just the theory, largely because it contextualizes application and the success or failure of that application.

The books mentioned above provide theory along with tips to guide leaders with various tasks; Collins includes several specific case studies to illustrate his concepts. However, not all are able to apply those theories and tips successfully. Ideally, an executive resigns or retires from his position on his own terms and on good terms with others around the organization. One needs only to pay attention to news regularly to read or hear of an executive who was fired or resigned under heavy pressure because of misdeeds or missteps. Certainly, much can be learned from a study of these cases.

The theory presented here emerges from reviewing news reports related to several cases of such experiences. Many of these reports provide specific messages from the executives as well as descriptions of actions that contributed to their resignation. In studying a number of cases and selecting cases to use for illustration in this book, I started with the search term "CEO President fired." I also applied the term "resigned under pressure." I, then, scrolled and read various listings, weeding out those who were fired or resigned due to illegal activities, ethical violations or poor financial performance of the organization. Through this process I hoped to draw the focus onto communication issues affecting the executive's forced exit. In a few cases, specific e-mail or speech artifacts were available to view how a message was communicated.

I rely on these news reports in my analyses. The analyses include going back to when the person was hired into the given executive position and reports that exist about the person's leadership style even before that. It is important to note that in each case, the person was hired with acclaim about their education and work background. In a few cases the person of focus combines an M.B.A. degree with a specialized professional certification or degree. They had clearly demonstrated a number of the items included in Collins' Level 5 Hierarchy. The news reports announcing the hire included mention of these. However, with one exception, each failed somewhere within the realm of expressing compassion. The news reports provide details about various messages the executives conveyed—either intentionally through e-mail or speech or public announcement and through multimodal modes of representation as well as messages the executives may have conveyed unintentionally. The executive may have been unaware of the message he or she sent. These messages are the objects of study—independently and holistically—within each case study; that is, these are what I analyze relative to the principles of Level 5 Hierarchy, emotional intelligence/rational compassion and related neuroscience.

In each case study, the executive encountered some kind of issue related to communication with an audience—either the board or lower management/workers—that contributed to his or her exit. In most of the cases, an external pressure existed; the organization needed to go through change, because the industry was experiencing change. The change was required not so much just to improve performance but to sustain existence and relevance. This complicates the context for communication.

Studies have reported that change causes the most stress in one's life. Books and articles describe ways to manage change; yet, it is still one of the more challenging dynamics to manage. In each case presented in this book, a communication dynamic—inconsistency between words and actions, inability to consider others' perspectives and respect them, or inability to explain decisions related to change—negatively affected trust in their leadership ability.

A few tried to enact changes that were not well received, in spite of the board's support. One did not respond appropriately via communication channels to a matter that was culturally sensitive. One was dismissed after several reports about their lack of patience and impersonal style. One was fired in what appeared to be a power struggle going on between people above them, only to be reinstated after considerable protest against the decision.

Organization of the Book

As indicated in the second paragraph of this chapter, leadership communication tends to involve a certain range of messages. Chapter 2 details the connections between neuroscience and emotional intelligence. Chapter 3 details the kinds of messages executives deal with and that particular cases in subsequent chapters address.

Each of the remaining chapters represents a particular case study. Communicating discipline and responsibility involves an awareness of one's own role in and responsibility to the organization and self-discipline. Communicating vision or goals requires strategic thinking, organization and collaboration. Communicating teamwork includes team-building, clearly defining roles/parameters, delegating duties, mediating and supporting work of others. Communicating context and knowledge means that one can speak intelligently about the market or industry and the economy. Executives need to communicate action related to decisions while inspiring change, which one cannot accomplish without having established trust from others.

Finally, there are lessons one can gain from differences in how women approach leadership and how men approach leadership. That is, leaders of each gender can apply some attributes generally associated with the other gender.

A caveat: There is considerable overlap in attributes of leadership as they pertain to communication. For example, one cannot enact change without having earned employees' trust that the change will work. While each chapter emphasizes a particular case, the reader should consider the chapters relative to the various situations presented and information available. Much as is the case with Collins' hierarchy one should not perceive that each item excludes elements of the others; the chapters work together.

2 The Neuroscience of Emotional Intelligence

In today's fast-changing world, facilitated by innovations in technologies, change to an organization and its employees' routine occurs on a regular basis. While leadership includes organizing people around tasks, most of leadership communication involves organizing and communicating change while facilitating smooth transitions.

As mentioned in Chapter 1, emotional intelligence is a way to facilitate such transitions and change by appealing more to the audience's feelings. Fear is among the emotions people feel when faced with change. How can one reduce this fear to make changes less daunting?

It's About Mirror Neurons

Mirror Neurons

Gallese et al. (2007) and Rizzolatti et al. (1996) first reported on the existence of neurons that appear to facilitate cognition of movements and behaviors that one observes another perform while doing a given task. Figures 2.1 and 2.2 show where these neurons are located in the brain, as mapped by Korbinian Brodmann (1909).

As I stated previously (2017), mirror neurons contribute to persuasion in that an audience wants to mirror some aspect of the speaker or the speaker may want to resemble some aspect of the audience to assimilate with it more. In this way, they act differently in persuasive exchanges than they do in instructional exchanges. Pillay (2011) notes that a persuasive message facilitates a shared experience between speaker and audience.

Further, Elzen (2013) acknowledges that, "These are emphatic mirror neurons. This means they cause us to experience the emotions felt by others simply by observing them" (paragraph 5).

Freedman (2013) reported the work of Marco Iacobini (2009). Summarizing some of it, he states that, "One of the central challenges in learning

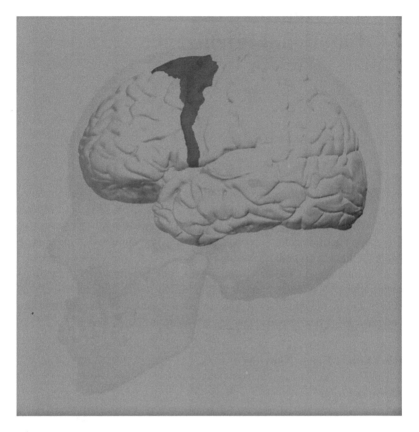

Figure 2.1 Brodmann Area 6: Mirror Neurons

Source: "BodyParts3D, © The Database Center for Life Science licensed under CC Attribution-Share Alike 2.1 Japan." (Google translate)

and leading is the ability for people to connect, to collaborate, and to find the common ground . . ." (paragraph 5). Iacobini (2009) describes findings associated with several different experiments by researchers related to mirroring behavior, empathy and perceptions of people about others. In each experiment a small group of subjects was placed in a room with one or more "confederates" (people who were not subjects but "planted" to evoke certain observable reactions to their behaviors) to help researchers with a certain task not related to the research topic. So, the subjects thought the researchers were looking for their perceptions of something, but they were focused on behaviors.

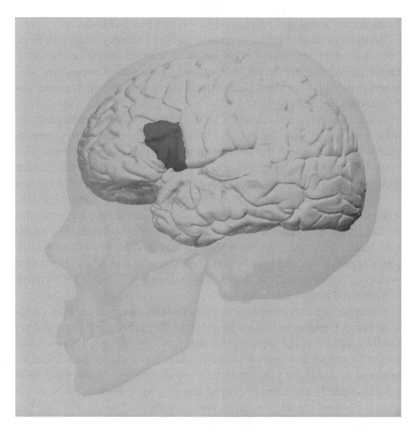

Figure 2.2 Brodmann Area 44: Mirror Neurons

Source: "BodyParts3D, © The Database Center for Life Science licensed under CC Attribution-Share Alike 2.1 Japan." (Google translate)

Summarizing the findings, Iacobini notes that subjects tended to imitate certain behaviors (rubbing their own nose or moving their foot) that the "confederates" made; subjects tended to like the "confederates" whose behaviors they imitated; and subjects tended to agree more with "confederates" who had similar perceptions of certain images that they had (pp. 658–659). He, also, notes that studies have found that mirror neuron responses are shaped by experience. Indeed, several studies find that, through neural plasticity (changes in neural connections over time); experience contributes to the development of neurons.

So, there is a biological connection between what people communicate through their words and actions and how others perceive them.

Between observing others' emotions and our tendency to imitate them, people need to understand what action to take to minimize emotional responses like fear in others. Elzen suggests, "Either avoid or minimise situations that trigger our stress mode or realise that tension within us may not be our own" (paragraph 9).

Acknowledging, with a mocking tone, that much work related to empathy alludes to mirror neurons, Bloom (2016) recognizes that mirror neurons enable one to "mirror" the feelings of another, but this is different from actually experiencing those feelings. This further distinguishes compassion from empathy (pp. 62–63). That is, one may see someone get hit in the arm with a baseball, but they cannot feel the exact same pain that victim feels. They may have been hit similarly with a baseball at one time and recall that feeling, but it may differ from the pain the victim experiences. The victim may have a lower pain threshold, the ball may have hit his arm with a different speed, or his arm may be more or less tender than that of the person watching. So, there is some shared emotion, but it is different for each person involved in the experience.

Likewise, the executive who needs to dismiss an employee may recognize that the employee will no longer have the same income and that her family may suffer; consequently, he may feel sorry for her. However, that executive cannot feel the exact same emotion the employee feels about the prospect of losing his job, unless he at some time was in the exact same position socially and economically as that employee. Further, an executive in that position cannot possibly experience the exact same emotions that each of the 200 employees he must dismiss as a cost-cutting move will feel about the job loss. Consequently, in such cases mirror neurons help us to sympathize with others more than empathize, according to Bloom.

Reward Neurons

Mirror neurons also can play a role in motivating others relative to sharing values about reward systems. Several studies related to dopamine, a neurotransmitter, recognize that the stimulated neurons are associated with perception of rewards and motivation. People will pay more attention to a message when rewards are so much as suggested. Advertisers integrate sex often into commercials, because it has shown to activate reward neurons. People pay closer attention when those neurons are activated. Reward neurons play into persuasive messages when a speaker acknowledges some benefit the audience may experience.

Figures 2.3 and 2.4 show where these neurons are located in the brain.

There are many ways one can experience a reward. A bonus or other financial reward is the most obvious in a business setting. However, it may also include feeling that one is part of a certain social group or team. All of these motivate one to respond a certain way because of the perceived reward.

Trafton (2016) reports that scientists have observed a relationship between reward neurons and decision-making and emotion. She states, "This finding expands the known decision-making circuit so that it encompasses . . . a subset of dopamine-producing cells . . . and integrates it to produce a decision on how to react" (paragraph 10).

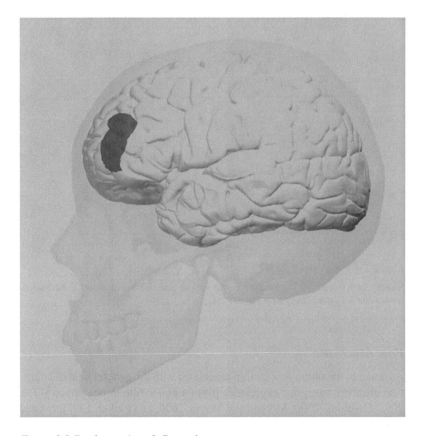

Figure 2.3 Brodmann Area 9: Reward

Source: "BodyParts3D, © The Database Center for Life Science licensed under CC Attribution-Share Alike 2.1 Japan." (Google translate)

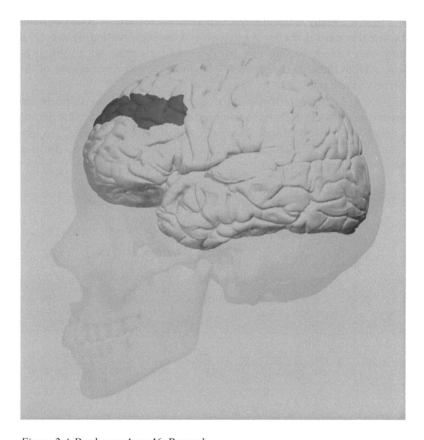

Figure 2.4 Brodmann Area 46: Reward

Prior Experience

As noted by Iacobini, scholarship associated with the general field of cognition observes that prior experience plays a major role in perception (Gee, 2003; Hutchins, 2000; Moreno and Mayer, 2000; and Pinker, 1997). I stated previously (2017):

> As one experiences a given situation, he or she recalls a similar experience and consequences associated with their actions related to it. If he did not like the outcome of his actions, he reflects on what he could

have done differently and changes his behavior accordingly to try to
get a better outcome the next time it occurs. With each experience, one
changes their actions to try to arrive at a favorable outcome related to
the experience. . . . These situations, though, tend to be social; so, this
attribute involves much social science. However, it also influences neurons, because neurons grow synapses with each social experience that
re-enforces certain information or knowledge. The more synapses one
has developed from previous experiences and learning, the faster one
can process related information.

(p. 36)

Such changes to neurons, stimulated by patterns of learning approaches,
contribute to affecting perception and attention attributes of information
processing.

Hutchins (2000) noted that cognition involves a system, which can include
neural systems or systems of groups of people (p. 2). Culture, derived from
a social system, also shapes our values; what we perceive as a reward, punishment; and what we value about other people and why we want to be like
them or not. Consequently, prior experience also contributes to development of reward neurons and mirror neurons.

Perspectives

Business students tend to learn about the concept of appealing to an audience by using "reader perspective," which focuses attention on the reader's
or audience's information needs and attitudes. Phrasing from the audience's
perspective, rather than one's own perspective, may be more effective. For
example, when someone wins a contest that includes a $200 award, he may
ask, "When will I get the check?"

One might phrase the response: "I sent that check out yesterday."

This example emphasizes the writer or speaker's perspective relative
to the situation. In effect, the speaker is stating that their responsibility
is completed. However, the audience may not know when to expect to
receive it.

In this case, reader perspective includes consideration of when the winner will receive the check. Using reader perspective, the message is: "You
should receive the check within the next two days." This message more
clearly responds to the winner's information needs.

So, empathy and emotional intelligence include some element of reader
perspective. The principle of reader perspective appears throughout this
book, and the formula engages it considerably. However, the formula also
allows for some elements of writer perspective.

Positive Language/Negative Language

As I indicated previously (2017), the way a message is phrased can affect not only how it is perceived but how the entire situation is perceived. If more space/time related to the message is spent on the positive attributes of the message or situation than on the negative, it can be perceived more positively than if it emphasized the negative aspects.

Which would you rather read or hear: "You need to improve efficiency; the projects you lead always wind up over budget." Or, "You work well with others and know your material; if you can improve efficiency, you will be able to reduce expenses and increase profit on those projects." The second emphasizes the positive attributes of the message, and you feel better about yourself and the situation.

Empathy and Performance

So, what does all this mean for motivating employees toward excellent performance? Gentry et al. (2016) researched this potential link and found that when employees perceive empathy from managers, they perceive the manager in a more positive light and feel better about performing tasks and in rating the performance of the manager (p. 4). The ways managers communicate with employees can affect morale positively or negatively.

Impact of Gender on Executive Communication Style

Plenty of articles, blogs and books describe differences in the way women and men differ with respect to leadership/management styles. Broadly, women tend to use a more cooperative style, seeking consensus through a democratic style, listening to various viewpoints and trying to come to some compromise across them. Men tend to use a more directive, command-like style. In this book, I present several cases of executive leadership failures that involve an almost equal number of each gender. However, the style women use tends to result in more favorable perceptions and responses from employees. The reasons involve the link between these cooperative, democratic styles and the neuroscience of emotional intelligence. Indeed, I have alluded to some of them as I discussed the various kinds of traits and how they may be communicated through words and actions in previous chapters.

In this section, I present these characteristics more explicitly toward identifying communication attributes that tend to be favored over other attributes. This information is important not just in terms of general leadership communication but also relative to specific audiences. Leadership style, including communication may need to adjust depending on the audience's gender characteristics and what kind of characteristics it values in leaders. If most employees are of a certain gender, they may prefer a certain kind of leadership over those valued by another gender. While these attributes are characterized relative to gender studies, either gender can apply them successfully in appropriate contexts. I detail scholarship related to gender communication styles and emotional intelligence relative to neuroscience principles; then, I apply the concepts to the case studies more specifically. As indicated in the Prologue, I had an enlightening and awkward experience related to gender and communication styles within my leadership development program. The results of one self-study within that program encouraged me to apply certain male-style attributes in a leadership context; when I did this in a setting that involved women, it was not well received. While somewhat humorous, reflection that applies these principles sheds light on why it happened.

Gendered Differences in Communication Style

Garfinkle (2016) notes that men and women differ in communication style relative to three different elements: general communication style, reward systems and self-branding. I detail the first two. Generally, he reinforces that women use a more democratic approach that involves more conversation and listening than men tend to use. Women, further, tend to encourage employees to find self-reward to motivate employees; that is, the employee will feel more valued somehow, but it is up to them to ascertain that way. Men, on the other hand, tend to use reward and punishment approaches, rewarding good work while punishing poor work. As such women tend to use a more "transformative" approach in communication, encouraging employees to find self-reward while seeing consensus; men tend to use a more "transactional" approach, using reward/punishment systems (Garfinkle, 2016).

Goman (2016) identifies three strengths and three weaknesses of male and female communication styles each. Among female strengths, she lists display of empathy and effective listening; among weaknesses in male style she lists insensitivity to audience reaction and bluntness. Among the weaknesses for women, she lists lack of authoritativeness, which she lists as a strength for males. Knight et al. (2015) note in their study of emotional intelligence and stress levels that female supervisors' highest median score, for empathy, happened to be the males' lowest median score (paragraph 30).

An observation that emerges from the case studies I provide is that in almost all cases, the male or female executive on which the case focuses lacked sensitivity to at least one of the main "teams" involved in the case while trying to be authoritative. That is, they communicated—either actively or passively, through words, actions or behaviors—a message that was deemed insensitive to the needs of a group with which they worked. In an effort to be authoritative, one may be perceived as blunt and insensitive. The word "authoritative" suggests command over a situation, and it also suggests respect and trustworthiness. This differs from "authoritarian," which suggests rigid discipline and forced obedience. One who commits to a decision and has others' trust and respect, because they were involved in the process or feel that their position was respected, is authoritative. One who commands others to do something without regard to their position or feelings, because they were not involved in the decision process, is authoritarian.

The Neuroscience of Gendered Communication

Digging deeper into scholarship on communication styles and gender, one can find studies reporting why these differences exist within neuroscience research. Case and Oetama-Paul (2015) report that women and men have different brain biology and are socialized differently, which affects neural development. Women are socialized to be more empathetic and respectful of others' feelings, while men are socialized to show power/authority and strength, which tend to translate to the transactional style attributes listed above.

Oxytocin and Trust

Baumgartner et al. (2008), Kosfeld et al. (2005) and Zak et al. (2005) observe that women have higher oxytocin levels than men and that oxytocin is linked to perceptions of trust in others. Oxytocin makes people feel more connected to others, suggesting that high levels of it would translate into being more sensitive to others' feelings.

Baumgartner et al. found that oxytocin moderates activity in the amygdala, thereby suggesting that trust reduces potential for fear. Once someone perceives another as trustworthy, they are less likely to fear that person will do something to hurt them. This may lead to the notion that once one has built trust, others may be more patient with them when they suggest change. Zak, Kurzban & Matzner found, using a "trust game" experiment, that rewards may be linked to increased levels of oxytocin in that oxytocin levels increased in subjects who received a monetary reward intentionally linked to trust.

The "trust game" experiment involves two people being paired separately, and the experimenter gives one a certain amount of money and tells that one to give the second some amount of money (even if 0), which the experimenter will triple. The second subject is asked to do the same with the amount he or she is given by the first subject, which the experimenter will triple. As one gives someone else some amount of that money, above 0, the other person feels some degree of trust in the first person, though there is some expectation of a return of money. Because of the trust created in the first exchange, the second subject gives some amount back, further increasing trust between the two.

This suggests links between reward neurons and trust from others. As one receives an award directly from another, they perceive that person to be trustworthy.

Assertiveness

While the literature strongly encourages managers and executives to exercise empathy, there is evidence that assertiveness can be helpful as well. Assertiveness is, generally, considered a male communication attribute. According to the Mayo Clinic (2017), assertiveness is an important communication skill; it helps to build respect from others, but it also can be respectful (paragraph 5). Being assertive does not mean being insensitive or aggressive. It means being clear, direct and decisive. One can convey a message assertively without being perceived as aggressive. This is the key to effective executive communication relative to being compassionate and not overly empathetic. Further, the Mayo Clinic states that being assertive can help to reduce one's own stress level.

Audiences: Perspective, Prior Experience, Mirror Neurons, Reward Neurons and Trust

I end this chapter with the identification of where many executives seem to go wrong with conveying a message. CEOs, unit directors, and executives are trying to meet the needs of at least two audiences generally. The board of trustees/directors is one of them. This is the group that hired the person in the first place, and the executive is trying to make them happy. They have risen to their board position through experiences that involved guiding organizations to financial and organizational success. They tend to emphasize the bottom line (generally measured by financial data) and spend much time reviewing financial data as a measure of success. They have accumulated some wealth because of it, too. They like others who have a similar perspective—that performance is measured by financial successes. These others have similar prior experiences, mirror their values, which emphasize certain rewards, and through these have gained the board members' trust. However, these differ from those of employees' perspective.

Employees may have experienced difficult times financially. They are the ones having to carry out changes that affect their job. They are concerned about keeping their job, because job loss may bring even more financial hardship. Consequently, they fear changes that may seem risky to them. Until they have full trust in someone who is trying to implement changes, those changes will be perceived negatively . . . and resisted.

This is where many executives collapse when they plan a given message relative to the different audiences—boards versus employees. They phrase messages more for appealing to the board, showing their allegiance and bond with the board—the group that hired them. As they do this, they forget the values and perspectives of employees, who perceive these kinds of messages to be forcing them to change; **this change may be more uncomfortable and riskier to them than it is to members of the board.** A series of messages that ignore employees' values will lead to distrust from employees. A message that ignores the board's values could lead to distrust from the board. Either can lead to being forced to resign under pressure or being fired.

Again, a rationally compassionate message can express consideration of others' perspectives and concerns while conveying the decision that most benefits the entire organization.

3   Leadership Messages

As indicated in Chapter 1, most literature in leadership communication studies identifies certain kinds of messages that executives and managers make on a regular basis. Collins (2001) integrates these to some degree in his hierarchy at different levels: communicating knowledge, communicating teamwork, communicating trustworthiness, communicating change and vision. I present in this chapter a summary of scholarship on each of these messages while linking some of the scholarship in neuroscience to them.

Communicating Discipline and Responsibility

Communicating responsibility involves two kinds of communication: communicating one's own responsibility to the organization and communicating to others their responsibility to the organization. When a leader communicates her own responsibilities, she is acknowledging her acceptance of her role as leader to the organization and willingness to act in that role toward bettering the organization. As one communicates others' responsibilities to them, she needs to make clear the parameters of those responsibilities, so employees know what is expected of them. Within these messages a certain tone emerges, reflecting emotional attributes of a relationship with the organization.

Responsibility of Leadership

Generally, a leader conveys his responsibility to the organization upon being appointed to the leadership position. Oftentimes, this is announced in the press release associated with the appointment. Most of the time, the message conveys what is obvious; his responsibility is to the organization and he is disciplined to meet that responsibility. Consider the messages conveyed by three of the leaders within the case studies. They are typical of such announcements.

Communicating Vision

Leaders need to be able to develop a vision for the organization and communicate it well. The vision itself is a plan for advancing the organization within its stated mission. Many articles acknowledge the importance of getting employee input in creating the vision itself. As stated in previous chapters, the more employees have input into any decision related to the direction of an organization, the more they will not only accept that decision but also support it. So, communicating a vision goes beyond "just" announcing that vision. It involves listening.

Developing Vision With Others' Input

Axner (n.d.) and Bates (2010) are among many writers who encourage leaders to seek input from employees regarding a vision. Bates lists listening at the top of her 4 steps to developing and communicating a vision. She suggests listening to personal stories of employees: "Personal stories are a rich source of material that can crystalize a vision" (paragraph 13). These stories, for example, may communicate successes as well as challenges, inspirational people and lost opportunities.

Axner points out the value of getting feedback from employees on a vision even after deciding on it. Listening to employees' responses will help you to understand how others may respond to your vision. This will, also, enable you to understand how you might phrase the message conveying your vision to a broader audience.

Again, inviting people to be a part of the vision development will help not only with creation of the vision but also with communicating it and getting people to buy into it.

Communicating Vision

Communicating a vision means not just telling employees about it but, also, in getting employees to buy into it and to understand their role in accomplishing that vision.

In most cases, conveying the vision seems like it should not be that challenging; however, as seen with some of the case studies in this book, a poorly communicated message may have severe results. Scarborough (Chapter 4) and Malone (Chapter 5) seem to convey the message in an "it's about me" way that alienates employees. Much as Malone actually does, both, basically, say to their employees, "I'm driving. Get on the bus, or I'm moving on without you."

Axner (n.d.) encourages leaders to help people buy into a vision by getting them to take some ownership of it. The listening one did as part of vision development can be handy with this buy-in. The stories one shared may be shared by others in the organization. The stories represent shared successes, frustrations and challenges. One can incorporate such a story into her announcement of the vision to recognize the input of others.

Generally, the more specific one can be in conveying goals and a vision, the more an audience can envision it and their role in accomplishing it. Several authors encourage identifying specific objectives and quantifiable measures of success. Decker and Decker (2015) encourage explicit connections between the stated vision and the audience's needs and how they will benefit. Such connections, also, reflect emotional intelligence by showing that one cares about the needs and desires of his team members/employees while establishing how the employees can contribute to attaining that vision.

Communicating Teamwork

> No one of us is more important than the rest of us.
>
> Ray Kroc

The Concept of "Team"

Organizational skill is an important element in managing a team. However, the quote by Ray Kroc above represents the essence of "team." The very concept means that everyone involved in a given task plays an important role toward attaining the successful completion of the task. Each member of a team has his or her own role and needs to be able to do it well. This teamwork involves communication in the sense that one needs to understand his role and what is expected of him in that role. This is part of organizational communication: helping people understand their job.

If one person on the team struggles, others may need to offer support or take up that person's work. This support, also, involves organizational communication. One needs to understand who can provide necessary support and communicate that to them, and one needs to be able to understand how to re-organize a team to take up someone's work.

As a team leader at any level in an organization, one needs to be able to communicate the concept of no one being more important than others on the team and a willingness to support others in their work. That can be repeated in meetings to reinforce it. It can be shown in various ways, not just in words. It contributes to a sense of trustworthiness from others. Anyone on the team can say to him or herself, "I'm important to our work, and I want to do well. If I need help, I know I can go to someone else without being judged and they will support me. We're all working toward a common goal, and we succeed or fail as a team."

Note here that I called attention to the emotional response of others on the team, even though this book is directed at the leader of the team. Again, emotional intelligence, while being partly about one's own understanding of their emotions, is also about others' emotions. I describe emotions leaders may feel, but it is important in a team setting to place others' emotions at least on the same level as one's own. The moment members of the team observe that someone else perceives their job to be more important than others' is the moment when trust begins to break down.

This message of "me as most important" is evident in a few of the cases presented throughout this book. We can consider a few of the facts identified in the cases of Scarborough, Malone and Mayer relative to their words as well as other modes of representation.

Another attribute of the concept of "teamwork" is supporting each other, even outside of the team environment. Plenty of texts describe how important it is to be supportive and encourage each other on a team. Offering each other assistance as needed shows support, as does offering a word of encouragement periodically and acknowledging when someone does something well for the team. A point often not treated relative to this supportive attribute is defending each other outside the particular team setting or when the team is challenged by another group. This may be evident in a sports environment. Consider how a batter's teammates come out of the dugout if the batter is hit by a pitch to offer support if a confrontation may arise because the pitcher's intention may have been to injure the batter. A coach might argue an official's call if he thinks it was incorrect, defending his players' play.

In a professional setting, one's team might be challenged by another team, and the leader needs to be able to step forward to defend their team. This will contribute to building trustworthiness. Others on the team will see that the leader is willing to defend them when they are challenged and recognizes the team members' value. The executive may be caught between two teams: the board and the employees. She needs to be able to step forward to defend each team as needed, while helping advance a program. This, further, reinforces that one must understand how to treat each team with rational compassion while, also, needing to negotiate between those teams.

In a couple of the cases presented in this book, one may see a group lose trust in someone because it no longer felt the executive was defending them or their position in the organization and, instead, was pushing another group's agenda on them.

Communicating Decisions/Change

There are many websites, books and articles that offer tips to manage organizational change and communicate about that change within the organization. Generally, these encourage such elements as conveying hope, listening to employees' concerns, inviting feedback, clearly conveying what the change is to be and talking about potential rewards among a list of others (Fenson, 2000; Johnson, 2017; Mulkeen, 2015; and Wagoner, 2017). I review a few of these here. However, I spend more time in this chapter presenting dynamics of the neuroscience involved, because of the point I made earlier: that executives are dealing with two different audiences—the executive team and board as well as the employees they lead. The different audiences react differently to change largely because of neural phenomena.

Change of any type brings with it stress. In fact, change is identified by most as the leading cause of stress. There is no shortage of evidence of this in empirical research. The American Psychological Association (2017) reports a variety of elements that impact stress, most of them related to changes in work or life dynamics. However, fewer studies describe why that is and why different people react differently to change. McEwen and Gianaros (2010) acknowledge that one's socioeconomic status has a large impact on how they respond to change.

The Neuroscience of Change and Socioeconomic Position

Wealthier and high-income people tend to respond less dramatically to change than those who are in lower-income positions (McEwan & Gianaros, paragraphs 7–8). People who have more money or are in better economic positions are less impacted by organizational change than are the employees who are in lower economic positions. This is due in large part to each group's previous experiences in life.

As mentioned in a previous chapter, various neurons are linked, and life experiences affect neural development. McEwan and Gianaros state:

> The hippocampus and amygdala are limbic brain structures that process experiences by interfacing with lower vegetative brain areas, such as the hypothalamus and brainstem, and higher cortical areas, particularly within the prefrontal cortex. They also help to interpret, on the basis of current and past experiences, whether an event is threatening or otherwise stressful—thus influencing allostatic responses. The amygdala is an essential neural component of the memory system for fearful and emotionally laden events.
>
> (Paragraph 21)

A few components of the neural system are identified in this passage, and I have discussed their relationship to persuasive messages previously (2017). However, it is important to note the links across them, their connection to fear (amygdala) and experiences (hippocampus).

Quickly reviewing, the amygdala is connected to very basic instincts associated with survival. Squirrels run to and up trees as a human walks by because of the fear they feel and embedded within their amygdala. Humans become anxious as they are about to experience something they have never experienced before, because of the basic instinct to survive; they don't know how dangerous that experience may be or what action to take to make it a safer experience. Once they have experienced it and know what to expect, they may be much less fearful of the event or actually welcome the experience. Change, generally, presents us with a new experience that we do not know what will happen.

The hippocampus is associated with memory, based on experiences. As humans learn through instruction and through experience, neural development increases and more activity occurs in the hippocampus. It is through our hippocampus that we recall events and how we reacted to them and we should react. As we experience something new, we have little to draw on from our experience; however, we may recall that we generally have had bad experiences with change or new things. That will come from memories stored in our hippocampus. People at lower ends of the socioeconomic scale may have had more bad experiences with change than those at the higher end.

While job changes are routinely identified as stress-causing events, consider that many leaders/executives have changed positions throughout their life. They may have been anxious about such a change early in their career, but they have experienced a number of changes by the time they are executives. Further, in almost all cases, they have sought those changes. Change, for them, is not as new or stressful as it may be for others. This is not the case for those in lower socioeconomic positions. Job changes may have meant lower pay and having to relocate their family. They have not sought such changes, but they have had to deal with them.

Further, executives have gained some degree of wealth and income that acts as a cushion should the change fail. As executives rise through the ranks their income increases—in some cases dramatically. By the time they attain an executive position, their income is likely at least in the six-figure range. This places them in the top 10% of society economically. They likely have invested quite a bit of their income in stocks and bonds. Should change fail and they lose their job, they may be safe for the few months it takes to find another job, or they may find a job quickly at a lower, but still high, income.

Most of the leaders identified in this book found high-paying jobs after they were fired or resigned, or they had considerable wealth by then. For them, even in being forced to resign due to leadership failure, they still have high socioeconomic status. Board members, generally, come from wealthier parts of society as well. Rarely do board members lose their position when a CEO fails. For someone on the lower end of the socioeconomic spectrum, change may mean losing his job and income, and he has little or no wealth to help cushion the loss. Many live paycheck to paycheck, and any loss of income may cause problems with other areas of life.

One becomes accustomed to routine, even on the job. Changes to that routine can cause stress, too, because they may impact job performance. If one's job performance declines, the threat of losing their job looms.

Communicating Change in Practice

All this means that one must treat the different audiences differently. Executives and boards may respond favorably to new ideas and changes proposed, because they know they have that economic cushion in case of failure. They need only be assured that the changes will deliver positive economic benefits, as reported in financial statements. The company/organization is healthy.

This changes as change is communicated downwardly to other employees. Again, upper-level managers may not be concerned, but lower-level employees will likely have serious concerns that need to be addressed. This is where emotional intelligence comes into play more. The more the message invokes compassion and recognition of others' feelings and fears, and need for hope, the better it may be received.

Communicating Trust

Much of what is covered in this book relates to building trust through compassion and empathy. At the most basic level, trust is the belief that someone supports, respects and has faith in you; they have your best interests in mind and will act on those. Employees feel more attuned with an executive/ leader who empathizes with them; they feel they can trust the executive to have their concerns in consideration as decisions are made and to support their work at multiple levels. As shown in the case studies in the two earlier chapters, as soon as one lost the trust of their employees or the board through action or inaction related to some form of communication, they were forced out.

As Beslin and Reddin (2004) state, "Trust is a powerful force that builds loyalty, increases credibility and supports effective communications. It gives you the benefit of the doubt in situations where you want to be heard, understood and believed" (paragraph 10). In each of the case studies presented earlier, the CEO or president lost credibility and the loyalty of the employees. In one case, they were lost from the board. Beslin and Reddin state further that, "At the heart of building trust is the process of communications" (paragraph 12). They go on to note that, in a 2003 study, half of employees who were part of a survey perceived that corporate communications about the company were not credible and were perceived by one-quarter to be dishonest (paragraph 12).

Parker (2015) even notes a connection between ways leaders respond to errors and trust. According to Parker, employees respond better to discussions about their mistakes if the manager addresses them respectfully and with compassion; doing so will result in them being more loyal to the manager and perceiving him or her to be trustworthy (paragraphs 9–11). Knowing that a manager is going to speak to them about a mistake they made creates a stressful condition for employees. If an employee trusts that a manager will "hear them out" and respond in a supportive way while trying to correct the behavior, they will feel better about the situation.

Compassion, even in uncomfortable situations such as talking about mistakes, can signal trustworthiness. A study by Knight et al. (2015) reinforces this statement. Connecting emotional intelligence to trust, they found that employees whose managers were perceived to have high emotional intelligence were regarded as more trustworthy than those who had low emotional intelligence.

This does not mean one must forgive all errors. Repeated errors may signal a problem with an employee, and this should be addressed. However, take each error/mistake individually and provide feedback that is positive while calling attention to the error and the need to avoid making it in the future.

For example, if an employee errs with a calculation or estimate, one might offer reassurance that it was a difficult calculation, show the right way to do it, and convey confidence that they can manage it in the future. If the error is repeated, the employee may need a refresher in certain kinds of calculations.

Collins (2001) does not suggest that one has high emotional intelligence as he develops his Level 5 Hierarchy, listing only that one is able to convey clear vision and goals and get people to work together (p. 10). Yet, emotional intelligence **and the ability to convey it** emerge as an important trait in these different cases. Further, such messages have to consider multiple audiences—employees as well as the board or other leadership group.

The rubric seen in Figure 3.1 provides some guidelines to help understand these considerations and their impact within multimodal communication contexts.

One can apply these to mode-specific messages. For example, Figure 3.2 offers another rubric to clarify attributes associated with a textual message.

In subsequent chapters, I examine particular connections between these cases and elements of leadership communication, including communicating discipline/responsibility, vision and goals, team-building,

Mode	Visual (what audience sees)	Aural (what audience hears)	Spatial (positioning relative to audience(s)	Appearance (what person looks like)
Superior	Inviting demeanor; open door policy; near employees; interacts periodically and regularly	Pleasant; Encouraging; positive tone	Comfortable Respectful near employees interacts periodically and regularly	Professional not too much better than others
Good	Inviting, open door policy	Pleasant Open, positive tone	Respectful, open to employees	Professional, a bit 'above' that of employees
Borderline Reasonable	Inviting official	Official Professional neutral tone	Official distance, may seem intimidating, respectful	Very official. much higher than others' 'position'
Needs Work	Intimidating	Official Angry disappointed	Hovers or too distant inaccessible	Very dressy professional while employees wear blue collar wear

Figure 3.1 Executive Multimodal Rhetoric Rubric

Compassionate Intelligence Level	Perspective	Prior Experience	Mirror Neuron Activation	Reward Neuron Activation	Trust-building
Superior	Very sensitive to others' views; explicit acknowledgement of consideration; acknowledgement of various perspectives involved. Reference to some statements of others	High consideration of others' experiences and recognizes value; reference to others' statements	High explicit recognition of values of all audiences involved experiences	Explicit acknowledgement of potential, specific reward valued by all audiences involved	Makes explicit connection between own experiences/ values and those of audience
Good	Somewhat sensitive to others' views; acknowledges others' input; summarizes some statements of others	Some consideration of others' experiences and implicit recognition of value; summarizing experiences	Reference to recognition of values in experiences	Explicit acknowledgement of potential reward valued by audience	Suggests connection between own experiences/values and those of all audiences involved
Reasonable	Suggests sensitivity to others' views by acknowledging others' input and consideration in decision process. Mentions types of narratives involved	Suggests consideration of others' experiences and implicit recognition of value in decision process. Mentions one experience	Reference to recognition of values in experiences	acknowledgement of potential, generalized reward valued by audience	Suggests connection between own experiences/values and an audience involved
Need to improve	Mentions others' input	No mention of consideration of others' experiences in decision	Generalized statement of something valued by audiences	Generalized statement of potential rewards	Little suggestion of shared experience/ values with audience

Figure 3.2 Executive Print-Linguistic Rhetoric Rubric

knowledge, action and change/adaptation, and trust. With each, I connect the communication challenge facing the executive to the Level 5 Hierarchy, review how the leader's messages—verbal and multimodal—invoked a negative response, and suggest possible alternative ways that the person could have applied elements of neuroscience, emotional intelligence and rational compassion to address a given situation or convey the offending message better.

4   Higher Education Case Study

Almost every industry is experiencing change as technology becomes more prevalent in the economy. The rate of technological innovation effects a need to change organizational behaviors and structure more rapidly. Consolidation of organizations within an industry also impacts how each organization manages itself. The person entering into a leadership position in such a climate enters a lions' den.

The leadership team—the alphabet soup of chiefs (CEO, CIO, CFO, COO, . . .) and vice presidents—needs to change the organization's culture and way of doing business generally. It is excited about remaining relevant and growing. It wants to see "results" of sustained existence and growth. It observes these through financial reports—perhaps the most basic reporting and measuring tool of any organization. For any for-profit organization, the measure of success is in the financial ratios. However, even non-profit organizations need to break even financially. Further, many non-profit organizations and institutions that were considered non-profit (e.g., educational institutions, hospitals, foundations) have shifted to a for-profit model. Growth cannot occur without revenues that exceed expenses. The drive to grow means generating more income than the organization spends—profit.

Profit comes through efficiencies. Increasing revenue by selling more or reaching more people/users of the product and/or services contributes to profit. Reducing expenses, also, contributes to profit. Increasing revenue while maintaining costs means changing some things in operations to increase productivity. This creates stress for workers/employees. Cutting costs, generally, means sacrificing resources available to workers/employees; this creates stress for those employees. One must do as much as they used to with fewer resources. Cutting costs may mean eliminating positions; this creates stress because people lose their job. When employees are fearful that they may lose their job at some point in the near future, their work is likely to be negatively affected. They cannot concentrate as well; they fear the next error they make will be used as an excuse to get rid of them.

Innovations, highly valued and encouraged in the general culture of today's business climate, come at the risk of losing money and time if an attempt fails. Yet, such losses are part of innovation. So, innovation may suffer. In such an environment, organizations may need to change how they operate; the general vision remains the same, but how it gets done differs from "business-as-usual."

Higher Education Case Study—Scott Scarborough

Scott Scarborough was hired as the President of the University of Akron in late June of 2014, replacing a popular president who had been in that position for more than 15 years. However, Scarborough would resign within 2 years, undone by communication issues related to his management of a $60 million "financial problem." Broadly, the communication challenge Scarborough faced, and in which he failed, pertains to Levels 1 and 3–5 in the Level 5 Hierarchy.

While he has the business background to gain the respect of the Board of Trustees, he lacks the experience in higher education that most of his employees have. This weakens his position relative to many of the employees he leads with respect to Level 1—technical knowledge within an academic field and related experience as a faculty member. He recognizes, reasonably, a need to shift vision and structure to remain competitive. He needs to communicate a change in organization relative to a change in vision while maintaining humility. This means that he needs to help employees see the need to change how the institution operates and motivate them toward that change without forcing it upon them unilaterally.

He maintains the favor of the Board and many in the business community; however, he loses favor with employees quickly. By the end of this chapter, the reader will understand what went wrong in communicating with employees and how some of the messages could have been conveyed better.

Professional Background

According to multiple sources, including the University of Akron's website (2014), Scarborough was trained in business and gained considerable experience in business, working in two accounting firms. Earning a C.P.A., he had strong certification as an accountant. He also earned an M.B.A and Ph.D. in strategic management as he rose to be an administrator at the University of Texas and, eventually, became the provost at the University of Toledo. A provost is the chief academic affairs officer of an institution, sometimes also holding the rank of vice president. Generally, this officer reports only to the university's president. While serving as provost there, he also held the position of COO at the University's medical college.

His various training in business and experience as an administrator at institutions of higher education helped him to garner considerable support from the university's Board of Trustees. Also pleasing to the Board was his ability to build trust with faculty in spite of his lack of academic faculty background. According to Biliczky (2014), Scarborough faced considerable skepticism in his ability to be a provost, because he had very little experience teaching or doing scholarly research, teaching a few classes as he held administrative positions.

The lack of teaching experience separated him from faculty relative to being able to empathize with them. Empathy is a large part of emotional intelligence, suggesting one can mirror another's feelings. The perception that one cannot do that is enhanced when one lacks experiences another has. That dissimilarity acts as a wall between them. Yet, Scarborough was able to win the trust of Toledo's faculty.

Once upon a time, administrators in higher education rose through the ranks of faculty and through levels of administration. After spending several years as a faculty member, one might become a department chair, for example; then, move on to become a dean . . . all the way to higher administrative positions, including vice president and president. Dr. Luis Proenza, the person Scarborough replaced, had been faculty in biology, studying neurophysiology, and rose through the ranks through different institutions as such.

More recently, such institutions have experimented with hiring business persons into ranking administrative positions; for example, some have hired former business executives into the position of dean of a college of business; others have hired business leaders as president (Basken, 2016). Also, many institutions now offer a degree program in higher education administration; graduates might move through that path. However, those paths were not well established in 2007, when Scarborough took the Toledo job. Those paths are still hotly debated in 2018.

Gaining Trust

Scarborough never taught classes or was expected to do scholarly research and publication—activities most faculty are expected to do. Consequently, he could not relate to faculty; so, how could faculty trust him? As Bilizcky reports, faculty found him to be engaging and respectful as well as supportive. He attended a faculty book club, and he talked about everyday topics there. Further, though a faculty member, who was part of the faculty union, had been trying for two years to address an issue with the University administration, Scarborough was able to reach a resolution favorable to the faculty member within a day of being involved with it. One can imagine how members of a union might respond to seeing an administrator get such favorable results so quickly.

One does not need a degree in neuroscience to understand how being able to talk to others about "common" topics might engage mirror neurons: "He's not so different from us after all." One could also understand that the ability to get the reward/outcome valued by the faculty union would endear him to the union: "Here's a member of management that actually supports us."

Such actions reflect a certain level of emotional intelligence. Understanding and respecting others' perspectives and putting them at ease are part of emotional intelligence. Further, note that communicating trustworthiness also involved action/behavior. He took action through behaviors to meet with people associated with the faculty union issue, and he resolved the matter himself—and did so quickly with material results.

Still, even after gaining that trust, he had to make difficult decisions that were not popular, as any leader must. Bilizcky reports that, even in his position prior to Toledo, faculty complained that he placed finances above academics. This seemed to be echoed at Toledo as well, where faculty had to increase their teaching load. Nevertheless, Toledo was able to move forward, and the UA Board of Trustees liked what it saw in him.

The "Financial Problem"

Within a year of taking the position at the University of Akron, Scarborough announced that the University budget was $60 million short. A number of dynamics contributed to this situation, for which the previous president and the Board of Trustees had been blamed. The University announced a plan that included $40 million in cuts, including faculty layoffs and the closure of some programs. This was not well received by faculty or the general public, though area business leaders called for patience to allow the changes to occur.

In an effort to help the public understand the situation and coming to Scarborough's defense, the previous president, Luis Proenza, explained various elements in the industry's business environment impacting the situation. Farkas (2015) reports that Proenza released a statement calling attention to a series of developments that many institutions experienced: enrollment decline calling for growth in programs, reduction in state funding for the institutions, changes in how the state funds institutions and updating campus facilities.

Indeed, in the previous 5 years generally across the country, institutions were having to cut or consolidate programs as funding declined and increase tuition fees to make up some of the difference, while many institutions found their buildings needed to be updated to handle new technologies and student culture. Few involved in higher education would debate the situation's existence, and none would be surprised that Akron had to take action. What would be surprising is the size of the shortfall and the speed with which Scarborough planned to address it—3 years.

Summarizing the steps Scarborough took to address the problem: He rebranded the institution, which was not a popular move publicly; he cut several positions, which created fear among employees; he cut some programs without much input from faculty; and he tried to develop a collaboration with a national technical college as that institution was failing.

Rebranding took the shape of including the term "Polytechnical University" to the institution's name. This was due, partly, to a movement in the country to link higher education to job skills, particularly in STEM disciplines (science, technology, engineering and math). Branding the University as such would explicitly make that connection. While he and the Board perceived this would raise the institution's identity to that of Virginia Tech and similar schools, this was perceived as reducing the identity to that of a smaller, less-esteemed institution. Allard (2016) reports that Scarborough felt the University needed this even as many around him were losing trust in him.

Cutting several programs with a single swing of the blade alienated him from faculty and the public. While other institutions had cut programs, none had done so much so quickly. He even cut the baseball program, deemed a money loser, alienating student-athletes. It also disturbed faculty, who suggested reducing spending on the football program (New, 2015).

Finally, Scarborough tried to forge a collaboration with ITT Technical Institute, a for-profit educational institution. This, too, was part of the effort to connect the institution more to "real world" education while increasing enrollment. As a collaboration with a technical college, students could move directly from their technical training to a degree program at the University. Such collaborations are not unusual; in fact, many institutions have such "articulation agreements." These agreements facilitate a smoother transition to a bachelor's degree program that many who earn a technical degree would not have because of a lack of certain coursework.

Teamwork: Audiences and Values

Even with the situation and developments, the Board praised the decisions and issued a message of support to the public. Knowing that the president had their support should alleviate some concerns; we are approaching this as a leadership team, and we trust his decisions. Their message and that of Scarborough recognized appreciation for faculty while acknowledging the need for such changes, extending the perception of "team" to faculty employees.

Magaw (2015) notes that the Board had faith in Scarborough's ability to turn the situation around because of Scarborough's successes at previous positions. He had saved one institution $4 million in a 2-year period, and he had improved the operating budget of another by $11 million in 6 months. Such successes would be valued by any on an executive board. They show immediate and valued results. However, their message was not valued by the public or faculty. Seltzer (2016) noted that many perceived that Scarborough did not understand the University's mission or respect academic values.

The public saga related to the lack of input from faculty and the alienation of graduates who still lived in the area wore on for about a year before Scarborough resigned. In spite of his previous financial successes, he had been known to disregard faculty while making quick decisions. The lack of faculty inclusion in these decisions caused lost trust. The cancellation of programs seemed to cause the public to understand that their institution was no longer theirs. Finally, a student started a petition on the website "Change. org" calling for his removal because of these as well as some activities that some perceived as conflicts of interest: naming others who had no professional academic background to his administration and outsourcing a nursing program to an organization on which he had once served as a board member.

The changes, while needed, were announced in a single message, without input from many who would be affected and would be implemented much too quickly to allow for change management. They showed a general disregard for the larger audiences' perspectives and emotions. They, also, showed some inconsistency between his goals to improve the institution and potential goals to enrich his associates.

Adopting a 5- to 8-year plan, including the various audiences that would be affected in the decision process and offering more than a generic "Thank you for your service" would have made the transition much more palatable. I am sure that the Board valued the speed with which the changes would occur and likely financial results. While Scarborough mirrored the Board's values, he was not mirroring others' values. In effect, he had placed the board's values above others'. Such a message immediately destroys any trust others had.

Discipline/Responsibility

Biliczky (2014) reported that in the initial hiring of Scarborough, he noted two specific responsibilities and commitment to them: "They (the trustees) want metrics . . . quantitative evidence" (paragraph 41–42), and "My first priority is to the people [at UA]" (paragraph 46). She also acknowledged that the chairman of the Board of Trustees stated that Scarborough would need to work with people in the community, especially in fundraising.

The easiest way to measure results is through quantitative data. It is why balance sheets, income statements and standardized tests among other such reports are used so often to assess or measure results. There are not many boards of directors/trustees that would not want to see such measurable results. So, this is, pretty much, an automatic responsibility: discipline to measurable financial results. He, also, states responsibility to "the people." Again, as a leader of a team, he would be responsible to this team. The people at UA represent the rest of the team.

It is interesting to note that it was the chairman of the board who acknowledged the third responsibility: fundraising beyond campus. Again, this is a primary function of the president of any academic institution. Many presidents would acknowledge it as their main responsibility, and some of the perks they receive are directly associated with facilitating such fundraising activity.

Their position comes with memberships (University-funded) to multiple clubs in the community. These may include country clubs, tennis clubs and other high-end clubs. While some may perceive this as a perk, the president is *expected* to network toward raising funds for the institution in these settings. Contrary to the perception many have of one relaxing or participating in light recreation, university presidents are, essentially, working while at those clubs. Some institutions maintain an office associated with helping the president recruit wealthy potential donors.

Finally, university presidents tend to live in luxurious homes, funded largely by the university or the university may provide a stipend to offset home expenses. This, too, is part of the fundraising responsibility.

So, this message only states the obvious but seems required. However, luxurious homes and swanky club memberships, also, send a message that the president is much different from employees. This can violate the "team" concept.

Scarborough/"Me"

Scarborough's "me" message is less evident than a couple of other cases in this book. Nevertheless, it became apparent when considering the snowball effect of a few such messages. Kelsey Watson, a student who initiated a petition at Change.org in 2016 to remove Scarborough as president of UA, lists in that petition several actions of Scarborough that suggest he perceives himself as more important than others. She lists 17 specific items. These include:

1. Cut more than 200 positions while ensuring that his friends are placed in leadership positions with significantly higher compensation than that of their predecessors,

2. Failed to honor the key concept of shared governance with faculty and students in administrative decision making, and
3. Unilaterally cut the men's baseball team to build a multi-million dollar "grand entrance" to the building that houses his office.

While Scarborough never explicitly states that he is more important than others, these actions suggest the perception that he is. The ability to make cuts to so many positions while still making administrative appointments at high compensation suggests power to make his own random decisions affecting the budget. He conveyed the necessity to make cuts, yet he is making appointments at higher salaries. This seems to suggest a forked tongue. His failure to consult faculty on key decisions is documented in previous chapters; however, Watson, as a student, makes the point that he also failed to consult students. Much as they have faculty advisory bodies, many institutions of higher education have student advisory councils representing the voice of students. Students are one of the main stakeholders in the work of education. So, their input is valued. Leaving them out of the decision process, also, suggests that they are less important than Scarborough is.

Finally, he cut the baseball program, yet, he builds a fancy entrance to the building that houses his office. While the cut may be much more than the expenses of the entrance, the linking of these two actions suggests that students perceive that he feels himself to be more important than the baseball program. Please note that it does not matter whether he does or does not perceive so; the actions make others perceive that it is so.

The message sent by his actions is that he is more important than others.

Key Takeaways

Understand and balance team expectations and cultures
Be inclusive where inclusivity is valued
Be consistent in mirroring team membership

The main issue in the Scarborough situation was not that a business person with administrative experience in higher education and very little faculty experience tried to lead such an institution. It was that he took a certain leadership style—leadership by directive—that may have worked in some business settings, but that was contrary to the institution's culture of inclusive leadership and slower change.

In certain business settings, one who is deemed to have superior knowledge of the business environment and skills to address the environment can simply declare a decision that seems to disregard others' perspectives. He or she may have the trust of others, who perceive that the leader has the best interest of the organization in mind and is doing what they can to do the right thing. Some understand that they may need to be cut on an at-will basis. That was not the case at the University of Akron, which was still used to a culture in which faculty had input in decisions at various levels that would be respected.

There were signs from his previous experiences that he placed business first and academics second. Surely, he had seen what he could and could not do in such a setting from his previous experiences. In each case in that experience, though, there was someone above him who, likely, had more academic leadership experience and could act as a buffer or mentor and say, "That may not work." One cannot please everyone on a team, especially the larger that team is. As provost at the University of Toledo, he led a team of faculty and other academic personnel. In some respects, he was able to win over their trust because of his actions, which communicated some level of empathy and support. However, some decisions were less well received, suggesting a business-first mentality.

Whether Scarborough perceived the time was right for him to act on his previous hunches without regard to others or caved to pressure from the Board of Trustees to act quickly to "get results," it is not known from reports I reviewed. Nevertheless, a primary lesson is not to disregard others' perspectives and rush change unilaterally *in a setting whose culture has not used that style*. I use italics there, because it may have worked in another setting in which people were used to that style of leadership. In the academic context, though, everyone felt alienated; and alienation is a quick path to distrust.

One needs to work with the Board but balance the Board's values with the values of the employees. As will be seen with a later case study, if a gap between the two sets of values exists, it may be more beneficial to favor the values of the employees over the Board's. However, it is possible to express appreciation of both perspectives. Further, an executive may need to explain to the Board a decision to implement a decision more slowly than it would like to implement it, especially related to a decision to change practice. The Board may like the decision to change but want to move forward quickly; employee groups may accept the change if it is implemented with their input and at a pace that allows them to adapt.

There was considerable resistance to the effort to cut programs, and the involvement of faculty in these decisions could have contributed to a very different message related to Scarborough's vision of addressing the $60 million "problem." While he may have set out to cut programs entirely, he may have found that faculty were receptive to reducing funding for certain programs or that faculty could come up with ways to increase student enrollment or address the cost issues. Because he did not include input from faculty, though, such a message could not occur.

With faculty input, he could have said, "In talking with faculty from the various programs of concern, we identified several ways to reduce expenses while trying to increase revenue. These include [. . .]"

Time to Adapt

Fenson (2000) notes that one of the more important factors related to change success is understanding how long it may take to change. She states, "Many leaders and managers underestimate the length of time required by a change cycle. That's why numerous reports indicate poor performance following many IPOs, mergers, change initiatives, etc." (paragraph 7). The timeline for the change should be conveyed to employees, and it needs to recognize a pace at which people can adapt emotionally as well as physically.

Scarborough's cuts were announced in a single sweeping message and would be implemented immediately. This would shock most who need time to absorb the information and potential impact on their own lives. Even including the statement that the University would help people find other employment is not as reassuring as it may seem. The message needs to be spaced out such that a general announcement about upcoming cuts is made some time before details are announced, which can facilitate meetings with those affected. This gives employees time to consider options, and it allows for input from employees about changes and transitions. This is followed some time later by the announcement of specific cuts, including the reassurance that others have been consulted and there is hope that the transition can be made with executive support. As the changes are implemented, one-by-one—not all at once—employees may come forward with positive experiences in that transition they have experienced, giving others real hope.

The Board's Message

It is interesting to observe how the Board presented the resignation publicly, because it considers some of the elements I encourage in this book: explicit references to consulting with others while, also, articulating a team environment. Seltzer (2016) reports that the Board of Trustees recognized the challenge Scarborough faced in changing the direction of the University as was needed. Even as Scarborough resigned, the president of the Board stated:

> We certainly considered the opinions of all the university's constituents. . . . They are all important. They all need to be together working in concert for the university to succeed so we found that it's best for new leadership to come into place to bring all the constituency groups to work together.

(paragraph 11)

Ultimately, while the Board's support for Scarborough demonstrated that they felt he was addressing their needs and values, the Board, essentially, recognizes that he is not addressing the needs of the faculty and other stakeholders. The last sentence acknowledges the balancing act required of such executives "to bring all the constituency groups to work together."

The Follow-Up

Scarborough took a faculty position, teaching strategic management at the University as part of his resignation agreement. Ironically, as of the writing of this book, he is now of faculty rank—one of the groups he seemed to ignore as president.

Matthew Wilson, a law professor who rose to become the dean of the University of Akron's law school, took over the presidency upon Scarborough's resignation. He restored much of what Scarborough set out to cut, while maintaining a positive relationship with faculty, the public and the Board. The institution still had the financial problem Scarborough acknowledged, but Wilson made some cuts that were less painful and reduced some costs; and, as of early 2018, it is easing out of the "problem" by dipping into cash reserves and increasing fundraising efforts.

In 2018, both Scarborough and Wilson applied for the presidency position at another institution. Scarborough did not make it far into the process, while Wilson was among the finalists for the position. Ultimately, Wilson was not selected to be that institution's president. A few weeks after the announcement of that institution's president, Wilson stepped back to faculty rank in the law school, citing health and family concerns. He resigned on his own terms.

5   Splitting Support

In the previous chapter, the case illustrated a clear separation between the values of the board and the values of others impacted by the leader's actions. In a number of respects, there was a wedge between the leader and one team he led that never would be resolved once a decision to make significant cuts was announced. The approach emulated a certain leadership style found in some business settings, which likely came out of Scarborough's business experience. While he had served as a provost, interacting with faculty on a regular basis, he was not able to convey and implement the changes needed in a way that faculty and others accepted. This failure to convey decisions effectively to faculty may have been due to limited faculty experience. While the change was necessary to respond to a financial problem, it required a different approach because of the culture in that setting.

In this chapter, I examine another case with several similarities to the one in the previous chapter, but this case also has several differences that need to be identified and addressed. One of the biggest differences, as is the case with several other chapters, is that the leader had considerable experience in the field and with the kind of people he led.

Unlike Scarborough's situation, the case in this chapter features a leader who had some support among some of the team members that he was leading, but not all. Some decisions went against a culture that was prevalent but that needed to change in response to the general business environment. People recognized this need to change, but the leader communicated several changes too quickly, destroying the relationship with a significant group within the employee teams he led. The board of executives recognizes his vision as appropriate and supports him, but the way he communicates it and its implementation rankle many who work under his leadership.

Health Care Case

Thomas Malone was hired by Summa Health System as its CEO in early 2015; he would resign under heavy pressure by January 2017. Broadly, the communication challenge Malone faced, and in which he failed, pertains to Levels 3–5 in the Level 5 Hierarchy. He recognizes, reasonably, a need to shift vision moderately and wants to do so by changing some structural elements to remain competitive. He needs to communicate a change in organization relative to that change in vision while maintaining humility. As with Scarborough, this means that he needs to help employees see the need to change how the institution operates and motivate them toward that change without forcing it upon them unilaterally. By the end of this chapter, the reader will understand what went wrong in communicating these and how it could have been done better. His biggest error is in communicating the change as unilateral; however, several multimodal communication errors are involved as well.

Professional Background

According to SummaHealth.org (2014), Thomas Malone earned his medical degree in pediatrics, working as a physician for several years before going on to earn an M.B.A. degree. Rising through the health care ranks, he eventually became Chief Medical Officer, then Chief Executive Officer at a medical school in Michigan. He took on a position as COO at another medical facility in Michigan before moving to a similar position at the Summa Health System in Ohio in 2013. After the long-serving CEO of Summa Tom Strauss retired at the end of 2014, Malone was selected to serve as the CEO of the System, starting January 1, 2015.

In early January 2017, he resigned under considerable pressure, much like that of Scarborough, demonstrating that even empathy with those one leads does not guarantee success as a leader. Indeed, even after having built relationships and trust from among the various employees of the System and the Board over that 2-year period prior to being selected to lead the System, it took only a few missteps related to communication and changes to destroy any trust many employees of the System had for Malone in short time.

Strauss had built an operation around the concept of a unified health care organization called "Accountable Care Organization" (ACO). The management approach brings physicians, hospitals and other health care professionals together to provide coordinated care while avoiding duplication of services and extensive bureaucratic paperwork, resulting in better quality care and financial benefits for all (Garrett, 2017). Within that structure, physicians still were able to maintain facilities outside the main hospital complex as a network of satellite facilities in various communities. Technology could facilitate coordination of care.

Malone continued this structure; however, he tried to bring it together physically, trying to close some care centers while negotiating tougher controls with physician groups. He had a couple argumentative encounters with physicians, asserting some authority of them. He, also, tried to impose a more-disciplined culture through a dress code. This rubbed several the wrong way.

There were three episodes that saw contentious exchanges with physicians. Garrett (2017) reports that one occurred very shortly after Malone's appointment as CEO. At a meeting of the medical leadership team, he was asked to clarify what he planned for his version of "population health," a broad term characterizing a perspective of health care for a group of people. According to Garrett, three people who attended the meeting acknowledged that Malone "told the group that he was now driving the bus and physicians had two choices—get on the bus or get off the bus. But the bus was moving forward with or without them" (paragraph 5).

Any such challenge would quickly bring about feelings of distrust; so, this would contribute to damaging any relationship he had with this group. Two more confrontations followed, one involving a lawsuit and another a public firestorm, explained below.

Among requirements of the dress code were natural-looking hair coloring and no visible tattoos and limited piercings. While rankling some initially, the policy was implemented with minimal backlash.

Even as he was trying to bring physicians together physically, he moved his CEO office from the main hospital, where personnel were used to having convenient access to the CEO, to another building over 2 miles away. This is a communication-related blunder in that it signals a separation of administration from the employees.

As that occurred, he seemed to fight against a physician group that wanted to open another facility. Physicians had been able to develop such groups and community care sites under Strauss, but Malone resisted. A lawsuit occurred over it.

Things came to a head when, late in 2016, the System broke away from a group of emergency room physicians with which it had been negotiating a new contract. While negotiations had been tense for a few months, starting in October, the year ended with the announcement that the System was moving on to another group. This set off bedlam.

Between the release of the physicians associated with the group, the group had been responsible for training medical students in ER care. Further, the new group contracted to serve the System's ERs was led by someone closely linked to Malone, suggesting a conflict of interest. Garrett (2016) reported that the new group is led by the husband of Summa's Chief Medical Officer, someone who would work closely with Malone on a regular basis.

The announcement came just before New Year's Eve, and the ER would not have enough staff without the physicians of the new group having some time to transition to the Summa ER system as the new year began. The new group tried, unsuccessfully, to recruit the physicians of the existing group so as to have the ability to staff the rooms. The new group even offered generous incentives in that recruiting effort.

Malone's trustworthiness was gone. By the end of that January, he resigned. As of 2018, Malone is a physician without administrative responsibilities at one of the Michigan facilities at which he was an administrator prior to his position at Summa.

Responsibility

In the release associated with Malone's appointment as CEO at Summa, he states, "Healthcare is evolving so rapidly, and all of us at Summa are up to the challenges. I look forward to continuing our successes" (Summa Health System, paragraph 5). The message is that the System has been successful, and he understands his responsibility to maintain that success in the face of changes to the industry.

Teamwork

As represented in the previous passage, Malone conveys a notion of team, using the pronoun "our" when referring to the System's successes. However, that message changes as he moves to invoke change.

Malone's "Me" message is evident not only in his words but also in his actions. As indicated, in a few meetings with physician groups, Malone actually states his importance, placing his decision above the values of those of the physicians: "I'm driving the bus." The message is easily and quickly perceived as "I'm more important than you." Consider that he could have said, "The bus is moving; make a decision to get on or stay off. . . ." Even as I would advise not to use that statement, either, that message has less of a "me" impact than his actual message. This is the obvious statement.

One of his actions as CEO of Summa Health System was to move the location of his office to another building, away from the main hospital. This action, also, tells others, "I'm different from you; I'm special." The move was not decided upon by the Board for some organizational reason; it was Malone's decision. Not only does he separate himself from his employees, but also he distances himself from them—by over 2 miles.

Communicating Change

Malone's message that he was "driving the bus" and others need to "get on" or "get off" means that he does not care how others feel about change; they need to adjust to him. Again, a simple message that conveys others' feelings and consideration will get a more favorable response: "In consulting with others, this is a change we need to implement, and employees/physicians have acknowledged that we may be able to implement it this way to make that transition easier." Knowing that peers had input in the transition planning and that those plans include consideration of their concerns helps to ease fears about transition.

One of the changes Malone implemented, changing the location of his office—a nonverbal message of change—served to create stress because he was no longer as accessible as previous CEOs were to employees. As indicated earlier, the new location was over 2 miles from where most employees were working. Implementing that change quickly offered no time for employees to adjust from the routine of being able to visit the CEO easily to having to use e-mail to contact him more often. Even as the change occurred, he should have acknowledged the benefits to the organization for that relocation and maintained an office at the hospital and shuttled between the two for a few months. The message is, "I'm going to be less accessible because I'm in charge here."

In word and action, Malone expresses that he is more important than anyone else in the Summa organization. These create a wedge between him and employees.

Using phrases that suggest the organization is a bus that is moving without others or that one is driving a bus rarely results in a positive response from an audience. Instead of saying, "I'm driving the bus . . .," Malone could have said, "I've talked to several physicians, and many are concerned about losing their affiliation with a particular nearby community. They acknowledged that they have a practice in [nearby city], trying to meet the needs of that community, which includes many who cannot drive to the main hospital. They wanted to know how to integrate their system into Summa while maintaining that connection to the community. We talked about two possible ways [. . .]"

That message is one that suggests that he listened to and heard the concerns of others and worked with them toward ascertaining possible solutions that could appeal to physician groups.

The Takeaway

Malone had considerable experience with the culture of health care; so, he could empathize with physicians and other personnel he led. Unlike Scarborough, he already had built trust and credibility among one of the main groups he led—physicians; this should have placed him well relative to emotional intelligence. However, he seemed to assume an authoritarian leadership style that was counter to the style with which many in health care were comfortable. This style became clear within his various messages—words and actions—in the first year of his tenure.

He asserted authority using strong words in several meetings with physicians; and he moved his office to a less-accessible place, physically and figuratively removing himself from the personnel he was leading and creating a visible gulf between him and them. With that development, others no longer trusted him.

6 Tech Company Case

Another case in which someone who was very much a part of the industry culture and rose through its ranks to become upper-level management is that of Marissa Mayer, former CEO of Yahoo. She was neither fired nor did she resign under pressure; her exit came as Yahoo was purchased by Verizon. Some note Yahoo's performance as a factor in her not being considered a good candidate to lead another company. Further, Mejia (2017) reported that she ranked among "the least likeable" CEOs in a survey. According to Mejia, this is due largely because of several communication-related issues, including a directive to bring many employees who were used to being able to work from home into the company's facility, habitually arriving late to meetings and micromanaging.

All of these communication issues seem to come out from her work ethic, which was generally praised and facilitated her rapid rise to upper management in the industry. As indicated in the Level 5 Hierarchy, work ethic is at Level 1, suggesting it is among the most basic attributes involved in leadership; however, it contributes to both her rise and fall. Weinberger (2017) summarizes her rise within the industry, noting that she often worked 100-hour weeks while teaching at Stanford (her alma mater) and not having much of a social life in college. Further, O'Brien (2016) reports that Mayer has been criticized for not taking enough maternity leave, typically using only a couple of weeks before returning to work. While very intelligent and technologically savvy, she lacked people skills outside of the executive board. These were apparent even in her work at Google.

Many high-level executives can probably appreciate that one needs to be able to "manage" a company seemingly 24/7. Even outside of the office, one represents the company to the public and is the "face" of the company. So, this work ethic, her technical savvy and skills and proven successes would be highly esteemed in the technology sector.

Background

Efrati and Letzing (2012) report on Mayer's initial appointment as CEO of Yahoo. They characterize the appointment as a coup for Yahoo, both in terms of poaching a successful executive from a rival company (Google) and in getting an industry-savvy engineer whose focus has been on the user's experience. They write that the board approached her; she did not actively apply for the job. The board, also, aggressively pursued her because of her track record. According to the board's chairman, Yahoo hired her because of her "unparalleled track record in technology, design, and product execution" (paragraph 17). Even Google's leadership expressed support for her as she transitioned to Yahoo (paragraph 21).

In summarizing her background with Google, Efrati and Letzing write:

> Ms. Mayer joined Google in 1999 and led many of its well-known products, including the look of the search engine. Most recently, she was responsible for initiatives related to local businesses and spearheaded Google's acquisition of Zagat, the business-reviews site [. . .]
>
> Ms. Mayer is known as a talented manager with an occasionally brusque style that can make her difficult to work for, according to people who have worked under her. She has an obsessive attention to detail, often micromanaging details down to the shade of colors in new product designs, these people say.
>
> (Paragraphs 29–31)

So, Mayer is well established not only as a knowledgeable engineer (lower levels of Collins' hierarchy) but also as a leader with vision who gets great results (higher level of Collins' hierarchy). Some have already noted her communication style, which suggests she may have some difficulty in a field that requires quick changes. These become more evident, and problematic, at Yahoo.

Missteps: Actions and Policy

Of the new policy regarding not working from home, Swisher (2013) notes that the industry generally allows people to work from home; so, such a policy was not well received at Yahoo, as reflected in a comment made by an employee noting the negative tone of the message (paragraph 9). This policy may have grown out of Mayer's own ethic of working at an office regularly and feeling that doing so facilitated the best environment for productivity and minimal distraction. This is evidenced in the message Mayer sent out via e-mail announcing the new policy. In that message she states that, "Speed and quality are often sacrificed when we work from home" (Swisher, paragraph 2).

Of her propensity to be late to meetings and value her own time, Carlson (2013) lists that she sometimes arrives a few minutes late, sometimes an hour late, and in some cases misses a meeting entirely. He even reports that, when she was at Google, she held "office hours" (a time period designated for impromptu or unscheduled visits/meetings with others) at which people (including VPs) had to wait outside her office, and she gave people five minutes each (paragraphs 11–12). Again, this seems to emerge from her work ethic.

Carlson notes that a reporter for *Psychology Today* observed that many people who have an all-consuming work ethic—as in they work tirelessly—lose track of time as they work on various projects or tasks. It is not so much out of disrespect to others (paragraph 20). Nevertheless, this can be perceived as lack of respect.

If one is occasionally late to a meeting, it may not be noticed, and few would perceive a problem with respect. However, consistently being late suggests that others' time is not valued. Holding "office hours" is not unreasonable, given a demanding schedule; however, making people wait and allowing only a few minutes with each suggests that their time and concerns are less important than one's own time and work.

Micromanagement is, generally, perceived as bad; because it suggests a lack of autonomy, trust in the quality of one's work and can slow processes. However, this can be connected to one's attention to detail, another attribute that many praised as Mayer rose through the ranks at Google (Weinberger, 2017; Oreskovic, 2015). As an engineer, one needs to have attention to details as they design something. Further, attention to detail is important when manufacturing the piece to ensure quality. So, such attention to detail is an excellent quality in an employee, especially a computer scientist.

However, people do not like to be micromanaged. So, this negatively affected emotional intelligence by suggesting a lack of trust in their work. It seems that even as she was leading product-design teams, Mayer was less an "emotionally intelligent manager," and more an authoritarian or autocratic leader.

Responsibility

The release associated with Mayer's appointment conveys her responsibility to innovation. "I look forward to working with the Company's dedicated employees to bring innovative products, content, and personalized experiences to users and advertisers all around the world." The company's statement in the same release reinforced that responsibility to drive innovation and excellence in customer experience and advertising revenue (Rushe and Arthur, 2012). Her job is to move the company forward in the fast-paced industry of Internet technology. She has had considerable success at Google, and the expectation is that it will continue at Yahoo.

Trust

The general nature of the trust Mayer had comes from her education and experience in the industry. Her educational background is in artificial intelligence/technology, and she was very successful at Google. So, she has considerable knowledge of the industry, and her successes give others a sense that they can believe in her ability to move the company forward.

Statements made by the Board reflect the trust they have in her due to her expertise and track record. Further, she has the trust of most of the employees because of that success as well, though some conveyed concern about another change generally. Few initially, at least, commented about her communication style.

Teamwork

Mayer's message is almost exclusively related to nonverbal actions. She shows up to meetings consistently late, or she flat out misses them. She, also, holds office hours at which employees must line up outside her office and get only a few minutes with her. Even if these are associated with a certain work ethic, which in many cases may be deemed admirable, in her position as CEO, they announce that she is more important than anyone else.

Others are, generally, expected to arrive to a meeting on time so it can start promptly and move in a timely manner. Others would be expected to give people, especially Mayer, as much of their time as the visitor needed. Distinguishing herself from these expectations sends the message that she is different; she is more important.

She may have arrived to meetings with the Board in a timely manner; no one who sat on the Board of Yahoo complained about her arriving late to meetings with them. It is likely that she never limited the time the Board had to meet with her either. As such, she mirrors their values on executive leadership priorities and meets their needs. Nevertheless, she places much less importance on similar behavior with her employees. Consequently, one may perceive that she prioritizes the leadership team over others that she is leading.

The Takeaway

Highly intelligent people who have a solid work ethic make for great employees and can drive innovations and productivity. However, technical skill/knowledge are not enough to ensure success as a leader. Communication drives management and getting people to do tasks. A lack of an ability to make people feel appreciated or respected negatively impacts success. It affects morale, which can affect productivity or create a sense of fear.

A piece of literature that is sometimes used in leadership training workshops includes an excellent reminder that what worked for one person may not work well for another; each needs to have a productive approach nurtured, but it needs to be customized to them. *Major Barbara*, by George Bernard Shaw, is about a Salvation Army leader's efforts to sustain work of the Army and her quest whether to compromise her beliefs in the work of the Army and her perception of her wealthy father's "donation" toward that end as an evil. Major Barbara is the Salvation Army leader. A particular character, Bill Walker, poses a unique challenge to her because he dislikes the work of the Army as charity, yet he himself lacks employment. Over the course of the plot, Walker roughly confronts Barbara even as she wants to help him. He seems to goad her as her father makes his pledge to help the Army, seeming to "buy" the Army off. She dislikes this approach to support the Army, since her father's business is in munitions—killing people. Nevertheless, Walker eventually impresses her father and her father hires Walker to work at his factory. Her father points out to her during a tour of his factory that Walker may not be using the "path" to "salvation" that Barbara perceives as ideal, but he is going down a "path" toward that end.

The lesson is that emotional intelligence recognizes that others may feel that autonomy may help people perform well because they are able to customize the means to an end to their own strengths. A rationally compassionate consideration would have included input from employees affected, and it would likely have led to a different message. For example, she may have been able to implement a policy wherein employees came into the office once a week or rotated throughout the week in a small group of offices shared by a few. Such a message, also, could convey her desire to have a closer connection to her employees in terms of physical proximity. Countering Malone's message of inaccessibility with the relocation of her office, she would be expressing potentially more accessibility to her. While she still had the office hours policy, she could interact with employees in passing in hallways, for example.

7   News Media Case

Jill Abramson was appointed Executive Editor at *The New York Times* in September of 2011, the first female to lead the newspaper. She would be fired from that position within 3 years. Less has been written about specific details related to messages influencing her ouster than of others; however, I provide as much as I can, based on available reports.

Broadly, the communication challenge she faced pertains to Levels 3–5 in the Level 5 Hierarchy. More specifically, based on information available, her gruff style never allowed her to get much support among her team members; she seemed to lack team leadership skills, contributing to an inability to motivate others effectively and with humility. While her initiative and work ethic helped her gain the trust of colleagues and executive boards in higher positions, it did not translate well once she was in a high-level executive position.

Like the others, she recognizes, reasonably, a need to shift vision and structure to remain competitive. She needs to help motivate others toward a change without forcing it upon them unilaterally. By the end of this chapter, the reader will understand what went wrong in communicating these and how it could have been done better.

Background

Educated at Harvard, she worked initially at an advertising agency. She became more actively involved in journalism in the 1980s, working as a researcher for NBC News. Working for a period at the *Wall Street Journal*; then, she was hired at *The New York Times* (NYT) in 1997 and appointed chief of the Washington Bureau in 2000 (Auletta, 2011).

Auletta reports that through diligent work and fearlessness in confronting co-workers' misdeeds, she developed considerable respect from her co-workers. While developing this respect, she also had the reputation of being short with people and, "Those who failed to meet her exacting standards were often berated, sometimes publicly; her critics thought that she played favorites and was mercurial" (paragraph 45). As she rose to Managing Editor, she, also, showed support for people, especially women, as they were promoted, hosting parties (paragraph 60). Male reporters did not like the attention she gave, but this was also during a period when fewer women worked at the NYT and there was an effort to do more to help them gain respect and equality.

A display of support goes a long way to communicating support. A "Good job" is nice, but "actions speak louder than words." One feels more appreciation with a celebration initiated by their supervisor. Auletta notes that her sense of empathy was valued (paragraph 52).

Even as this support came, though, some still perceived her negatively because of her brash style. Nevertheless, she was able to gain some experience with web-editing as technology in journalism moved more online. This background gave her more experience toward understanding the industry and changes that would be needed. Indeed, upon being named to the Executive Editor position, she would find that the NYT was doing poorly financially and needed to respond to changes in the industry toward doing more with digital media.

Shortly after this experience, she was appointed to be Executive Editor. Auletta reports that in the interview for the job she identified her brash communication skills as a weakness and said she would work on them. Based on reports after her firing, she did not do well in addressing them.

Problems

Auletta (2014) reports that, in addition to some internal disagreements about how to move the NYT forward, she still approached communicating with others in a brash way. Byers (2014), also, reports that her communication skills contributed considerably to her being fired. Quoting the NYT's publisher, Arthur Sulzberger, Byer writes that Sulzberger listed several concerns:

> Including arbitrary decision-making, a failure to consult and bring colleagues with her, inadequate communication and the public mistreatment of colleagues . . . [and that if they were not addressed] she risked losing the trust of both masthead and newsroom.
>
> [. . .] Ultimately I concluded that she had lost the support of her masthead colleagues and could not win it back.
>
> (Paragraphs 8–9)

Emotional Intelligence and In-Fighting

Auletta (2011 and 2014) reports that even as she had gained the trust of others because of her emotional intelligence, her style of communication often created visible messages that made her seem brash, which would be received negatively in general.

In spite of her extensive knowledge of the industry, successes at various levels of leadership and having gained the trust of many with whom she had worked, things fell apart largely because of the various messages conveyed in multimodal forms of communication. The statement from Sulzberger above identifies no fewer than four:

1. "Arbitrary decision-making," which suggests a lack of consistency in behavior;
2. A failure to consult and bring colleagues with her, suggesting a failure in teamwork and considering others' perspectives;
3. Inadequate communication, which may mean brash phrasing/tone; and
4. The public mistreatment of colleagues, which is a visual form of communication; even if directed only at the one person, others can see it and perceive a generalized statement.

As in the other cases, a leader's communication style was poorly received, contributing to distrust among the people she led. While she was a veteran of the industry and had garnered considerable respect among her peers prior to her leadership role, in the position of leadership, employees perceived her harsh style as destroying morale and leading them not to trust her. The messages were not conveyed just through words, either. By not seeking input from colleagues and keeping them informed of moves, they felt out of the loop and alienated. Further, even more negative messages were perceived as she accosted colleagues publicly, losing their trust.

Once again, while the Board may have supported the executive initially, recognizing her expertise and skill in moving the company forward, employees lost trust in her. Through rational compassion she may have been able to minimize the effect of decisions with which her reporter-colleagues disagreed. At the same time, it is difficult for one who seems to perceive the executive's role as "bus driver" to make such accommodations.

One gets the impression that it may be better not to say anything at times, given the amount of trouble some seem to get into with their actions and words. However, inaction and lack of words can also cause someone to be fired, as in the next case.

8   Advertising Agency Case

When an employee sends an e-mail that could be perceived as racist, the CEO needs to do something about it quickly. This includes communicating with leadership internally, any external leadership and employees. It also involves taking certain action, where certain groups/teams may perceive a certain action is more appropriate than other action.

When he found out that an employee had sent an e-mail that some employees perceived as racist, Jim Palmer, CEO at Campbell Ewald, an advertising agency headquartered in Detroit, Michigan, and owned by Interpublic Group (IPG), spoke to the employee immediately, according to Coffee (2016a and b) and Bruell (2016). Nevertheless, Bruell (2016) and Stein (2016) report that he evidently did not inform the leadership team at IPG about what had happened and did not terminate the particular employee, which is the action the IPG leadership felt appropriate. That was enough for him to be fired in January 2016.

The Level 5 Hierarchy elements featured in this chapter are at Levels 2 and 3. Palmer tries to make an executive decision, but he leaves one team important to that decision out of the decision process. He fails to communicate with that group, leading to lost trust and resulting leadership failure.

Trust

Palmer had worked in advertising for 2 decades when he was appointed to the position. So, he came with considerable experience and knowledge of the industry. This contributes to the trust the Board would have in him.

In essence, this case involves poor choices by 2 leaders: one a team leader, and the other the CEO. In October of 2015 a white creative director at the agency's San Antonio office sent an e-mail inviting his team members to participate in "Ghetto Day," for unknown reasons. Coffee notes that the e-mail included the statement that, "Ghetto music, Malt 45s at lunch, and of course, drugs and prostitution are legal all day until close of business. Word, my cerebral gangsters."

The message includes a photo of two African-American men standing on a sidewalk of an urban street with a "Pabst Blue Ribbon" beer sign in the back and trash lying along the sidewalk near the road. "Colt 45" is a malt liquor manufactured by Pabst Brewing Company. "Word" in this context may be used as the slang for "telling the truth," a term often associated with rap music. References to drugs and prostitution may be perceived to be references to stereotyped black ghetto culture.

The photo (Figure 8.1), shared publicly in Coffee's (2016b) report, is titled "Chicago Ghetto.jpg" in Wikimedia Commons and dated May 1974. Looking further, the photo was taken by John White, a Pulitzer Prize-winning photojournalist, "documenting African-American life on Chicago's South Side" as part of the Environmental Protection Agency's photodocumentary program in 1973 and 1974 (Wikipedia, John H. White). The program was an effort to document "subjects of environmental concern" (Wikipedia, DOCUMERICA).

So, the team leader/creative director, perhaps as a joke or effort to be funny as part of an effort to bond with his team, sent the message with the photo. However, between the image and the words used in the message, there is a clear potential for the message as a whole to be perceived as racist.

Figure 8.1 Photo in Controversial E-mail

"Chicago Ghetto.jpg" public domain; from Wikimedia Commons

Team Communication

From reports, Palmer spoke to the creative director shortly after it happened and sent an announcement denouncing it as not representing the agency's values. This sounds like it would be enough to set things right, as it represents direct action taken within the employee-related team environment. However, not contacting the IPG leadership team to consult about a range of actions to take alienated them from the decision process.

The IPG leadership team needed to know that such an incident happened, and, it appears, wanted to have input into what action to take. Clearly, it would have fired the creative team leader immediately. So, while the action Palmer took may have seemed productive between the particular team leader and Palmer, addressing the problem internal to that team setting, the "other," leadership team needed to be included in the decision on what action to take. In this case, the executive left out the higher-level team that appointed him.

After the incident had been reported in an industry publication, the agency lost an account. So, the impact went well beyond the agency itself. Once again, the CEO excluded a team from a decision process; this time, though, it was the leadership team itself.

The Takeaway

This case reinforces the need to communicate something to the Board, even if it is just to acknowledge plans to address a problem. Rather than convey what he would do, Palmer omitted the Board entirely from the decision process. He should have acknowledged the issue to them, conveyed what he was planning to do and invited their feedback on it. He would have acted in a way with which they agreed. Even if they had agreed with his original decision, they would have been included in that process. That, also, would mitigate Palmer's liability in any lost accounts because of the action taken.

While he would need to disappoint the creative team leader with the firing decision, a rational, compassionate approach would have enabled input from both sides—Board and employee—and led to a better organizational consideration.

9   Mary Beckerle Case
A Happy Case, Depending on Perspective

I have provided five examples of leadership communication failures. I have one more case study to present, but it differs dramatically from the others for two reasons: It features three executives—each at different units within a single larger entity; it shows that support from multiple audiences can lead to success even in the face of adversity, and it shows the value of trust. In the five cases already covered, someone was either fired or resigned under pressure, be that pressure from the Board or from the employees of the organization. This chapter features the cases of a president of a university trying, with someone who was a CEO of a health care unit linked to that university, to fire the director of a research institute in that health care unit. This one move and the reasons for it, which would soon emerge, led to the "higher-ups'" resignations.

More is known about the director affected, so I detail her position in this case, as well as that of the health care unit's CEO. However, I call attention to the messages sent by the two executives who resigned under pressure; they were the executives who represent the failure valued in this set of cases.

Case

Mary Beckerle was fired by a group overseeing the work of her unit, the Huntsman Cancer Center at the University of Utah. The University president and the health care unit's CEO fired her. However, after considerable backlash for this decision, from employees as well as from a major donor, she was reinstated. The major donor and employees had considerable respect and trust in her, and they recognized that her superiors were dismissing her for reasons unrelated to her performance. They were losing trust in the executives who made the decision to fire her.

While the director was reinstated, the health care unit's CEO would resign, and the University president would move up his retirement. This case illustrates various issues embedded with communication within the Level 5 Hierarchy. As with most of the other cases in this book, much of it occurs at Levels 3–5. The health care unit CEO wanted to bring about a change in vision, but she was unable to do it within a team environment. She did it unilaterally and in a way that suggested a character flaw—the desire for power over others.

Background

Vivian Lee was educated at Harvard, earning an M.D. in radiology before working at Duke University and New York University's Medical Center. After earning an M.B.A at NYU, she rose to become a vice dean at the NYU Medical Center. Within 5 years of completing the M.B.A. degree she was appointed to the position of the health care unit's CEO at the University of Utah. She earned several awards throughout her career, earning considerable respect from colleagues.

After earning a bachelor's degree in biology, Mary Beckerle earned a Ph.D. in Molecular, Cellular and Developmental Biology, and the University of Utah hired her to teach in their Biology Department (Vandersteen Bailey, 2017). She quickly rose through academic ranks, even earning enough respect from her superiors and others at the University of Utah that she was persuaded to stay when offered a position at Johns Hopkins. The University was in the process of building a cancer research institute, which appealed to her. She would be appointed the Institute's director, and she has held that position since 2003 (Vandersteen Bailey).

Over the course of more than a decade, she earned further accolades, publishing extensively and serving on several health care–related boards. These all contributed to establishing her as a respected scholar among the colleagues whom she directed at the Institute. Like a few other cases presented earlier, she "rose from the ranks" to a level of leadership.

All seemed to be going very well for the Institute, in fact, when a power struggle erupted over the Institute's funds and control in early 2017. Stuckey (2017a) reports that the University president and the University's health care CEO wanted to take over the Institute, which had been operating independently.

Through a series of e-mails, Beckerle was informed that she would be forced out of her position (Stuckey, 2017a; Stuckey and Wood, 2017; and Servick, 2017). The announcement was met with considerable outcry that the University was making the wrong move, and many recognized the power struggle shortly afterwards. However, it was through the intervention of the major donor, Jon Huntsman—the Institute's founder and "biggest benefactor"—that the dismissal would be undone (Stuckey, 2017a and b). Awkwardly, the President moved up his planned retirement, and the health care CEO resigned shortly after the incident.

Responsibility

Lee's vision of the health care unit at Utah was to increase operating efficiencies—a task that seemed to make her many enemies while still being supported by higher-ups. It appears that this vision may have contributed to the situation, with her wanting to unite the operations, including funding, of the Institute with that of the entire unit.

Beckerle's responsibility was to lead the Institute, and its performance under her leadership had proven success. As indicated in the background subsection, she had published scholarship and was active in service. The faculty she supervised, also, were active and productive.

Trust/Teamwork

Through her education and early success as faculty, Beckerle had earned a reputation for being successful. Her colleagues, clearly, respected her and trusted her leadership. She conveyed her trust in them as well (Vandersteen Bailey, 2017).

Lee had also earned trust from many of her colleagues due to her many awards and scholarship. Stuckey and Tanner (2017) report that many of her colleagues at the unit thought highly of her.

The Power Play

David Pershing was the President of the University of Utah. In early 2017, there was a dispute related to the funding relationship between the University and the Institute. The Institute is affiliated with the health care unit, of which Lee was CEO, but operated as an independent small business unit therein. The University supported the Institute with funding, but the Institute also had its own fundraising activity as well. It appears that the University withheld funds that it was supposed to give to the Institute as part of an effort to weaken the Institute financially and force it to be more dependent on the University, so the University could gain more control over it. This was challenged by the main donor/founder of the Institute, Jon Huntsman— after whom the Institute is named. Lockhart and Chen (2017), though, suggest that Lee also presented information to Pershing that the Institute was not performing well in fundraising efforts.

Stuckey (2017a) and Lockhart (2017) present the e-mails that demonstrate this effort. One, in particular, shows the intent to take control of the Institute. Stuckey reports that Pershing "wondered if there were a way to agree to Huntsman's demands to continue funding from the University but take total control of all cancer operations within the university. I mean so Mary really works only for you," Pershing wrote to Lee, "and we somehow also get control of the fundraising" (paragraph 3). Lockhart reports that Huntsman believed Lee wanted to use the Institute's general funds (University-funds and own fundraising) across other health sciences as well (paragraph 16). Huntsman would not support that. Stuckey and Tanner (2017) report that Lee's vision was to unite most of the health science units. So, this effort may have been initiated by her, and Pershing's message reflects his agreement with her vision, while also agreeing that the funding dynamic be part of that vision.

It appears that Lee was the one who pushed for Beckerle to be fired, perhaps to remove what she perceived to be an obstacle to attaining her vision. Pershing and the University's board supported that decision, and Pershing sent the termination letter to Beckerle via e-mail.

Through the reporting of these messages, others became aware of the intent of the higher-level executives. Pillay (2011) notes that mirror neurons help us to understand the intention of someone else (p. 63). Even as one interprets a verbal message, one is able to understand the speaker's/writer's intention with a certain amount of information available. While the firing, initially, was perceived as mysterious or strange, as the messages emerged, the intention to gain more power became evident. This caused others to lose trust in these executives.

Indeed, Pershing apologized to Huntsman in an October 2017 letter, acknowledging regret at not consulting with the Huntsman Foundation about the disputed funding. While the letter may be perceived as an effort to save face publicly, it acknowledges a broken trust. While the effort may have been initiated by Lee, Pershing went along with it and failed to consult a Board related to the decision. Again, Pershing moved up his retirement because of the incident, staying on to facilitate a smooth transition to the next University president.

Lee resigned immediately after the e-mails were released publicly. Stuckey (2017b) reports that she had fired someone else at the health care unit at about the same time as Beckerle's firing, and that person was able to be reinstated as well. Stuckey and Tanner (2017) report that many were afraid of Lee, even as she was a respected scientist. She serves on several boards of directors.

The Higher-Level Leadership Loses

This is the only case presented in this book in which the leadership group above that of the particular executive who was fired lost its reputation and was forced out. The power struggle reflected poorly on them, and a conflict between them and the major donors, without whose funds the Institute would not be able to function, emerged. Ultimately, the voice of the major donors (which represents another "team" associated with leadership for non-profit organizations, equivalent to shareholders for a corporation), along with the support of her faculty-colleagues won out.

A better way to handle the effort to merge the Institute's work into that of the health care unit would have been to collaborate with the upper-level team of the Institute—the Foundation, including the major donor, toward an agreement. It appears like those discussions may have occurred in initial phases, but there may have been some push-back, eliciting the Pershing e-mail to Lee to give them what they wanted while moving control under the University's purview. Lee should have used the opportunity to make her case for merging the two, without speaking negatively of Beckerle.

While Lee had Pershing's support, likely because of the trust he had in her, Pershing should have met with Beckerle to ascertain her side of the story regarding the fundraising concerns Lee had raised. Not allowing Beckerle that opportunity gave the appearance that he was ignoring an important voice that should have been part of the team communication.

Further, the e-mail message Pershing sent to Lee regarding Beckerle "working only for you, and we somehow also get control of the fundraising" is difficult to interpret as anything other than a power play when taken by itself. When the lack of communication with Beckerle and the Foundation is combined with that e-mail message, the total message seems to be that he had total faith in Lee's vision and reporting while lacking a similar trust in the others affected.

Finally, Pershing's omitting the Foundation from the decision irked an important funding arm of the Institute and, by extension, the University. The University's Board supported the firing, but quickly recognized the problem. It was after a meeting among the Board, Pershing and Lee that Lee announced her resignation, effective immediately; and Pershing announced his plans to move up his retirement. So, at that meeting the Board must have expressed concern about the public's perception of the situation, perceiving it had lost faith in the University administration—in the persons of Pershing and Lee—and decided it best to move forward without them in those positions. In the meantime, the two firings Lee made that seemed to be unreasonable were reinstated.

Tough Lessons

A lesson that emerges is that one should be careful about which team(s) they are trying to appease. Again, one is likely to disappoint an audience with a difficult executive decision. However, a rationally compassionate message—one that includes acknowledgment of various perspectives involved—can allay potential for lost trust. In most cases, winning the trust of the larger team (employees) as well as that of the Board will lead to success. In this case, though, it was a power struggle at the top that was the issue, and others lost trust in those people because of the self-serving nature of their actions.

Conclusion

Throughout this book, I have presented failures in executive forms of communication—in their words and in other forms of communication—and explained what contributed to their failure in terms of concepts that have been favored in executive development circles. Using these examples and showing how they may have been corrected, I hope the reader has come to understand the delicate balancing act associated with the executive position and how messages can be managed with a compassionate approach.

Indeed, rather than present an entirely new theory or conception, I have built on existing theories espoused in leadership studies, using them as a foundation on which to build an approach to applying a reasonable means of formulating a message that has the challenge of meeting the needs of multiple audiences, including what is best for the organization one leads.

Economic Impact of Compassion

Boards have a focus on a set of numeric data that show performance measures. Employee morale affects productivity (Seppalla and Cameron, 2015; and Weakliem and Frenkel, 2006). Further, Bowles and Cooper (2009) assert that there is a positive relationship between high employee morale and various measures of financial performance (p. 59). So, the messages one conveys, visually, orally, spatially and in combination of these, can affect organizational performance in many ways.

Socioeconomics, Neuroscience and Rhetoric

As indicated, one's socioeconomic position can affect how they perceive a given executive decision. One who has a financial cushion does not fear the same kinds of hardships that one who has little cushion fears.

As I mentioned earlier, most of the leaders identified in this book have found high-paying jobs after they were fired or resigned or had considerable wealth by then. Scarborough moved into a faculty position that still pays him over $150,000 annually. Malone returned to a Detroit hospital at which he once held an executive position and resumed his position as a physician, likely earning over $100,000 annually. Mayer's compensation package with Google and Yahoo provided her with several million dollars in salary and stock options. Vivian Lee moved to a tenured faculty position at the University of Utah, and she was able to maintain her $1 million per year salary for the year after her resignation. So, they did not experience the kind of poverty or impact on their lifestyle that lower-level employees would have felt had they lost their job.

One's disposition to change is affected by neuroscientific elements that are part of one's biological makeup. The executive who understands how to consider these items relative to the different audiences—boards and employees—will be perceived as compassionate. Even as some disagree with a decision, they may respond more favorably and feel better about it if the message conveys respect for their position than if the message seems to ignore it.

Applying the rubrics to the messages shown, one can see how they would be received negatively. The rubric in Figure C.1 shows more specific examples of the impact specific messages would have.

Just as important as learning from successes, we can learn from failure. Executives need to be aware of the various ways they communicate, consciously and unconsciously, to various audiences, and they need to consider how to convey the message that the audience needs in order for those employees and/or board members to understand and respond as the executive wants them to respond.

With this book, I have demonstrated how synthesizing principles encouraged in leadership development programming and integrating consideration of the neuroscience behind the rhetoric therein while carefully critiquing failures in leadership communication like those in the cases presented in this book can help executives understand not only what to do with the message—in its various forms—but also how to do it and why.

Superior	We spoke with [audiences] and we found that many were concerned about [x and z]. One person told us about when they… [story]. Another acknowledged [story]. A third said, [story].
	These stories are important because they show how people have treated [x and z].
	They suggested …as a way to address those issues. One person suggested [specific suggestion]; another suggested [specific suggestion].
	In considering these perspectives and their input, we will implement [y], because it balances [a and b—perspectives/concerns].
	We will implement this over the next few [period of time] to allow for a smooth transition. We did something similar when I was at [previous workplace] and it was successful, because….
	[audience a] may expect to [action toward change]. [audience b] may expect to…
	This should lead to increased profit of 10%, which may translate to salary raises ranging from $2000 to $5000 for audience a and $4000-8000 for audience b.
Good	We spoke with [audiences], and they are concerned about [x and z]. An example of one person's story is: [story].
	That person suggested we address it by…
	Others suggested addressing those by…
	While we thought about these concerns, we will implement [y] over the next [period of time]. This should balance those concerns while allowing some time for adjustment.
	When I was at [previous workplace] we did something similar, using…[similar approach], which helped make things easier.
	We expect this to increase sales by 10%, which could lead to pay increases of 2-6% for audience a and 4-8% for audience b.
Borderline Reasonable	We spoke with [audiences], and we found that most are concerned about [y]. They suggested addressing this by…[summarize suggestions]
	Given their input, and to facilitate a smooth transition, we will implement [y, which coincides with suggestion] in the next [period of time].
	This will increase revenues by 10% and may help to increase salaries for audience a by 3% and for audience b by 6%..
Needs Work	We spoke to [audiences], and they think…
	We will implement [y] over the next few months. This will enable us to meet our sales goals and continue to succeed.

Figure C.1 Executive Rhetoric Impact Rubric

References

Allard, Sam. (2016). University of Akron is no longer 'Ohio's Polytechnic University'. *Scene*, May 20, 2016. www.clevescene.com/scene-and-heard/archives/2016/05/20/university-of-akron-is-no-longer-ohios-polytechnic-university. Accessed March 5, 2018.

American Psychological Association. (2017). Stress in America: Coping with change. *Stress in America™ Survey*. www.apa.org/news/press/releases/stress/2016/coping-with-change.pdf. Accessed February 28, 2018.

Auletta, Ken. (2011). Changing times: Jill Abramson takes charge of the Gray Lady. *The New Yorker*, October 24, 2011. www.newyorker.com/magazine/2011/10/24/changing-times-ken-auletta. Accessed February 19, 2018.

Auletta, Ken. (2014). Why Jill Abramson was fired. *The New Yorker*, May 14, 2014. www.newyorker.com/business/currency/why-jill-abramson-was-fired. Accessed February 19, 2018.

Axner, Marya. (n.d.). Developing and communicating a vision. *Community Toolbox*. https://ctb.ku.edu/en/table-of-contents/leadership/leadership-functions/develop-and-communicate-vision/main. University of Kansas. Accessed February 23, 2018.

Basken, Paul. (2016). U. of Akron chief's resignation ends Rocky presidency. *Chronicle of Higher Education*, June 1, 2016.

Bates, Suzanne. (2010). *How Leaders Develop and Communicate a Vision*, April 19, 2010. www.bates-communications.com/articles-and-newsletters/articles-and-newsletters/bid/57961/how-leaders-develop-and-communicate-a-vision. Accessed February 23, 2018.

Baumgartner, T., Heinrichs, M., Vonlanthen, A., Fischbacher, U. and Fehr, E. (2008). Oxytocin shapes the neural circuitry of trust and trust adaptation in humans. *Neuron*, 58 (4), 639–650. doi:10.1016/j.neuron.2008.04.009.

Beslin, Ralph and Reddin, Chitra. (2004). How leaders can communicate to build trust. *Ivey Business Journal*, November–December 2004. https://iveybusinessjournal.com/publication/how-leaders-can-communicate-to-build-trust/. Accessed February 20, 2018.

Biliczky, Carol. (2014). New UA president takes helm this week: Has history of wasting no time with tough decisions. *Akron Beacon Journal*, June 30, 2014.

Bloom, Paul. (2016). *Against Empathy: The Case for Rational Compassion.* New York: Ecco.

Bowles, D. and Cooper, C. (2009). Why morale is so important. In: *Employee Morale.* London: Palgrave Macmillan.

Bradberry, Travis and Greaves, Jeanne. (2009). *Emotional Intelligence 2.0.* San Diego: TalentSmart.

Brodmann, Korbinian. (1909). *Comparative Localization Theory of the Cerebral Cortex: Illustrated in Their Principles on the Basis of Cell Construction.* Leipzig: Barth. http://digital.zbmed.de/zbmed/id/554966. urn:nbn:de:hbz:38m:1-1298.

Bruell, Alexandra. (2016). IPG fires Campbell Ewald CEO Jim Palmer. *Ad Age. com*, January 29, 2016. http://adage.com/article/agency-news/ipg-fires-campbell-ewald-ceo-jim-palmer/302413/. Accessed February 19, 2018.

Byers, Dylan. (2014). Why Jill Abramson was fired. *Politico.com*, May 17, 2014. www.politico.com/blogs/media/2014/05/why-jill-abramson-was-fired-188718. Accessed February 19, 2018.

Carlson, Nicholas. (2013). Marissa Mayer is late all the time. *Business Insider*, January 23, 2013. www.businessinsider.com/marissa-mayer-has-a-bad-habit-of-being-late-all-the-time-2013-1. Accessed February 18, 2018.

Caruso, David R. and Salovey, Peter. (2004). *The Emotionally Intelligent Manager.* San Francisco: Jossey-Bass.

Case, S. S. and Oetama-Paul, A. J. (2015). Brain biology and gendered discourse. *Applied Psychology*, 64, 338–378. doi:10.1111/apps.12040. Accessed March 2, 2018.

Clarke, Sandy. (2018). Is empathy a bad decision-making guide for leaders? *Leaderonomics.com*, February 9, 2018. https://leaderonomics.com/leadership/emotional-empathy-leaders. Accessed February 18, 2018.

Coffee, Patrick. (2016a). Campbell Ewald's CEO has been fired amid fallout over a staffer's racist email. *AdWeek.com*, January 29, 2016. www.adweek.com/brand-marketing/campbell-ewalds-ceo-has-been-fired-amid-fallout-over-staffers-racist-email-169291/. Accessed February 19, 2018.

Coffee, Patrick. (2016b). Campbell Ewald fires CEO Jim Palmer after 'Ghetto Day' email controversy. *AgencySpy.com*, January 29, 2016. www.adweek.com/agency spy/campbell-ewald-creative-invited-team-to-celebrate-ghetto-day/101194. Accessed February 19, 2018.

Collins, Jim. (2001). *Good to Great.* New York: Harper Collins.

Decker, Kelly and Decker, Ben. (2015). Communicating a corporate vision to your team. *Harvard Business Review*, July 2015. https://hbr.org/2015/07/communicating-a-corporate-vision-to-your-team. Accessed February 23, 2018.

Efrati, Amir and Letzing, John. (2012). Google's Mayer takes over as Yahoo chief. *The Wall Street Journal*, July 17, 2012. www.wsj.com/articles/SB100014240527 02303754904577531230541447956. Accessed February 28, 2018.

Elzen, Katrin Den. (2013). Emotional intelligence and mirror neurons. *Daretosayyes.Com*, August 21, 2013. http://daretosayyes.com/emotional-intelligence-and-mirror-neurons/. Accessed March 20, 2018.

Farkas, Karen. (2015). Former University of Akron President Luis Proenza blames fiscal woes on state cuts, enrollment declines and the need to expand. *Cleveland. com*, August 17, 2015.

Fenson, Sarah. (2000). 10 tips for communicating change. *Inc.*, June 1, 2000. www.inc.com/articles/2000/06/19312.html. Accessed February 20, 2018.

Fernandez-Araoz, Claudio, Roscoe, Andrew and Aramaki, Kentaro. (2017). Turning potential to success: The missing link in leadership development. *Harvard Business Review*, November–December 2017, 86–93.

Freedman, Joshua. (2013). The neuroscience at the heart of learning and leading. *Forbes*, May 8, 2013. www.forbes.com/sites/ashoka/2013/05/08/the-neuroscience-at-the-heart-of-learning-and-leading/#559c7e9667df. Accessed March 20, 2018.

Gallese, V., Eagle, M. N. and Migone, P. (2007). Intentional attunement: Mirror neurons and the neural underpinnings of interpersonal relations, *Journal of the American Psychoanalytic Association*, 55, 131–176.

Garfinkle, Joel. (2016). Difference between male and female leadership. *Career Advancement Blog*, August 1, 2016. https://careeradvancementblog.com/male-female-leadership. Accessed March 1, 2018.

Garrett, Amanda. (2016). Summa health bringing in new doctor group to staff its ERs starting new year's day. *Akron Beacon Journal*, December 31, 2016. www.ohio.com/akron/writers/summa-health-bringing-in-new-doctor-group-to-staff-its-ers-starting-new-year-s-day. Accessed February 17, 2018

Garrett, Amanda. (2017). Examining the two-year tenure of Dr. Thomas Malone, Summa CEO and president. *Akron Beacon Journal*, January 15, 2017. www.ohio.com/akron/business/healthcare/examining-the-two-year-tenure-of-dr-thomas-malone-summa-ceo-and-president. Accessed February 17, 2018

Gee, J. P. (2003). *What Video Games Have to Teach Us About Learning and Literacy*. New York: Palgrave McMillan.

Gentry, William A., Weber, Todd J. and Sadri, Golnaz. (2016). Empathy in the workplace a tool for effective leadership. *Center for Creative Leadership*. www.ccl.org/wp-content/uploads/2015/04/EmpathyInTheWorkplace.pdf. Accessed March 22, 2018.

Goman, Carol Kinsey. (2016). Is your communication style dictated by your gender? *Forbes*, March 31, 2016. www.forbes.com/sites/carolkinseygoman/2016/03/31/is-your-communication-style-dictated-by-your-gender/#8c04e26eb9d3. Accessed March 2, 2018.

Helios HR. (n.d.). A review of workplace leadership styles: Men Vs. women. *Helios HR* (Website). www.helioshr.com/2015/06/a-review-of-gender-leadership-styles-common-traits-in-men-vs-women/. Accessed March 2, 2018.

HR.com. LEAD. (2018). *Award winners* (Website). www.leadershipexcellence anddevelopment.com/content/lead2018-award-winners. Accessed February 14, 2018.

Hutchins, E. (2000). Distributed cognition. *IESBS Distributed Cognition*, May 18, 2000. www.artmap-research.com/wp-Content/uploads/2009/11/Hutchins_Distributed Cognition.pdf. Accessed June 22, 2012.

Iacobini, Marco. (2009). Imitation, empathy, and mirror neurons. *Annual Review of Psychology*, 60, 653–670.

Jenson, Anabel. (2017). 20 outstanding books on emotional intelligence that could change the world (2017 update). *EQ Business, EQ Life, EQ Parenting*, March 12.

90 *References*

Johnson, Elisbeth. (2017). How to communicate clearly during organizational change. *Harvard Business Review* (Website), June 13, 2017. https://hbr.org/2017/06/how-to-communicate-clearly-during-organizational-change. Accessed February 20, 2018.

Knight, J. R., Bush, H. M., Mase, W. A., Riddell, M. C., Liu, M. and Holsinger, J. W. (2015). The impact of emotional intelligence on conditions of trust among leaders at the Kentucky department for public health. *Frontiers in Public Health*, 3, 33. doi:10.3389/fpubh.2015.00033.

Kosfeld, M., Heinrichs, M., Zak, P., Fischbacher, U. and Fehr, E. (2005). Oxytocin increases trust in humans. *Nature*, 435 (7042), 673–676. doi:10.1038/nature03701. Accessed March 2, 2018.

Levitt, Steven D. (July 28, 2008). From good to great . . . to below average. In: *Freakonomics*, New York: William Morrow.

Lockhart, Ben. (2017). 'Mounting mayhem': Emails show discontent over differing visions from cancer institute, U. Brass. *Desert News*, August 5, 2017. www.deseretnews.com/article/865686162/Emails-show-clash-between-Huntsman-Cancer-Institute-CEO-U-administration.html. Accessed March 23, 2018.

Lockhart, Ben and Chen, Daphne. (2017). Dr. Vivian Lee resigns post at University of Utah. *Desert News*, April 28, 2017. www.deseretnews.com/article/865678822/Huntsman-executive-says-faulty-report-influenced-Beckerle-firing.html. Accessed March 23, 2018.

Magaw, Timothy. (2015). University of Akron to slice budget by $40M, cut 215 jobs. *Crain's Cleveland Business*, July 10, 2015.

Mayo Clinic Staff. (2017). Being assertive: Reduce stress, communicate better. *Mayo Clinic* (Website), May 9, 2017. www.mayoclinic.org/healthy-lifestyle/stress-management/in-depth/assertive/art-20044644. Accessed March 2, 2018.

McEwen, B. S. and Gianaros, P. J. (2010). Central role of the brain in stress and adaptation: Links to socioeconomic status, health, and disease. *Annals of the New York Academy of Sciences*, 1186, 190–222. doi:10.1111/j.1749-6632.2009.05331.x.

Mejia, Zameena. (2017). Why Marissa Mayer is the 'least likable' CEO in tech. *CNBC*, May 31, 2017. www.cnbc.com/2017/05/31/why-yahoo-ceo-marissa-mayer-is-the-least-likable-ceo-in-tech.html. Accessed February 18, 2018.

Moreno, R. and Mayer, R. E. (2000). A learner-centered approach to multimedia explanations: Deriving instructional design principles from cognitive theory. *Interactive Multimedia Electronic Journal of Computer-Enhanced Learning*, 2.

Mulkeen, Declan. (2015). Effectively communicating change to a disgruntled workforce. *TalentCulture* (Website), January 19, 2015. https://talentculture.com/effectively-communicating-change-to-a-disgruntled-workforce/. Accessed February 20, 2018.

Mulvey, Kelsey. (2017). These are Amazon's top-selling books on business management and leadership. *Business Insider* (Website). Accessed February 13, 2018. February 21, 2017, 6:33 PM. http://www.businessinsider.com/best-selling-business-management-leadership-books-amazon-2017-2

Murray, Alan. (2010). *The Wall Street Journal Essential Guide to Management.* New York: HarperCollins, p. 11.

New, Jake. (2015). Cutting the wrong sport? *Inside Higher Ed*, July 20, 2015.

O'Brien, Sarah Ashley. (2016). Marissa Mayer on maternity leave: 'I understand I'm the exception'. *CNN.com*, May 6, 2016. http://money.cnn.com/2016/05/06/technology/yahoo-marissa-mayer-maternity-leave/index.html. Accessed February 18, 2018.

Oreskovic, Alexei. (2015). Yahoo insiders say Marissa Mayer is an indecisive micromanager and may be looking to quit. *Business Insider*, November 19, 2015. www.businessinsider.com/yahoo-insiders-criticize-marissa-mayer-management-2015-11. Accessed February 18, 2018.

Parker, Clifton B. (2015). Compassion is a wise and effective managerial strategy, Stanford expert says. *Stanford News* (Website), May 21, 2015. https://news.stanford.edu/2015/05/21/compassion-workplace-seppala-052115/. Accessed February 28, 2018.

Pillay, S. S. (2011). *Your Brain and Business: The Neuroscience of Great Leaders*. Upper Saddle River: Pearson/Financial Press.

Pinker, S. (1997). *How the Mind Works*. New York: W.W. Norton and Sons.

Remley, Dirk. (2017). *The Neuroscience of Multimodal Persuasive Messages: Persuading the Brain*. New York: Routledge.

Rizzolatti, G., Fadiga, L., Fogassi, L. and Gallese, V. (1996). Premotor cortex and the recognition of motor actions. *Cognitive Brain Research*, 3, 131–141.

Rushe, Dominic and Arthur, Charles. (2012). Google executive Marissa Mayer to become Yahoo CEO in surprise move. *The Guardian*, July 16, 2012. www.theguardian.com/technology/2012/jul/16/google-marissa-mayer-yahoo-ceo. Accessed March 5, 2018.

Seltzer, Rick. (2016). Acrimony at Akron. *Inside Higher Ed*, June 1, 2016. www.insidehighered.com/news/2016/06/01/controversial-president-leaves-university-akron. Accessed February 20, 2018.

Seppalla, Emma and Cameron, Kim. (2015). Proof that positive work cultures are more productive. *Harvard Business Review*, December 1, 2015. https://hbr.org/2015/12/proof-that-positive-work-cultures-are-more-productive. Accessed March 16, 2018.

Servick, Kelly. (2017). Power struggle erupts at Utah cancer institute over director's firing. *Science*, April 20, 2017. www.sciencemag.org/news/2017/04/power-struggle-erupts-utah-cancer-institute-over-director-s-firing. Accessed March 5, 2018.

Shaw, George Bernard. (1907). *Major Barbara*.

Stein, Lindsay. (2016). Campbell Ewald names CEO to succeed fired Jim Palmer. *Crain's DetroitBusiness*, April 20, 2016. www.crainsdetroit.com/article/20160420/NEWS/160429985/campbell-ewald-names-ceo-to-succeed-fired-jim-palmer. Accessed March 5, 2018.

Stuckey, Alex. (2017a). Newly released emails show University of Utah president sought 'total control' of Huntsman Cancer Institute. *The Salt Lake Tribune*, August 14, 2017. www.sltrib.com/news/education/2017/08/12/university-of-utah-president-sought-total-control-of-huntsman-cancer-institute-before-fight-with-the-prominent-family-came-to-light/. Accessed March 5, 2018.

Stuckey, Alex. (2017b). Head of neurology at University of Utah reinstated after he was axed by Vivian Lee. *Salt Lake City Tribune*, August 16, 2017. www.

sltrib.com/news/education/2017/08/15/head-of-neurology-at-university-of-utah-reinstated-after-he-was-axed-by-vivian-leebr/. Accessed March 23, 2018.

Stuckey, Alex and Tanner, Courtney. (2017). U. health care CEO Vivian Lee resigns after cancer institute controversy. *Salt Lake City Tribune*, April 29, 2017. http://archive.sltrib.com/article.php?id=5231822&itype=CMSID. Accessed March 23, 2018.

Stuckey, Alex and Wood, Benjamin. (2017). Huntsman says University of Utah 'power grab' is behind firing of acclaimed researcher from cancer institute top post. *The Salt Lake Tribune*, April 19, 2017. http://archive.sltrib.com/article.php?id=5189972&itype=CMSID&page=2. Accessed March 5, 2018.

Summa Health System. (2014). Summa Health System appoints Thomas Malone, M.D., as President and CEO. *Summa Press Room* (Website), November 17, 2014. www.summahealth.org/pressroom/allnews/2014/summa%20health%20system%20appoints%20thomas%20malone. Accessed March 3, 2018.

Swisher, Kara. (2013). 'Physically together': Here's the internal Yahoo no-work-from-home memo for remote workers and maybe more. *AllThings.com*, February 22, 2013. http://allthingsd.com/20130222/physically-together-heres-the-internal-yahoo-no-work-from-home-memo-which-extends-beyond-remote-workers/. Accessed February 18, 2018.

Trafton, Anne. (2016). Newly discovered neural connections may be linked to emotional decision-making. *McGovern Institute for Brain Research at MIT*. http://mcgovern.mit.edu/news/news/newly-discovered-neural-connections-may-be-linked-to-emotional-decision-making/. Accessed March 20, 2018.

University of Akron. (2014). Dr. Scott L. Scarborough named UA's 16th President. *UAkron.edu* (Website). www.uakron.edu/alumni-friends/akron/news-detail.dot?newsId=d4bfef7c-52ac-40f9-838c-1683ee40eb41&pageTitle=Recent%20Headlines&crumbTitle=Dr.%20Scott%20L.%20Scarborough%20named%20UA%27s%2016th%20President. Accessed June 1, 2018.

Vandersteen Bailey, Elise. (2017). Mary Beckerle: 'Very fortunate conductor of a world-class orchestra'. *VLCMtech.com* (Website), July 19, 2017. http://blog.vlcmtech.com/vlcm-foundation/mary-beckerle-very-fortunate-conductor-of-a-world-class-orchestra. Accessed March 5, 2018.

Wagoner, Heather. (2017). Communicating change. *The Blog Huffington Post*, July 17, 2017. www.huffingtonpost.com/heather-wagoner/communicating-change-the_b_11031100.html. Accessed February 19, 2018.

Watson, Kelsey. (2016). Scott Scarborough must resign or be removed as President of the University of Akron. *Change.org*. www.change.org/p/the-university-of-akron-board-of-trustees-scott-scarborough-must-resign-or-be-removed-as-president-of-the-university-of-akron. Accessed February 20, 2018.

Weakliem, David L. and Frenkel, Stephen J. (2006). Morale and workplace performance. *Work and Occupations*, 33 (3), 335–361. doi:10.1177/0730888406290054. Accessed March 16, 2018.

Weinberger, Matt. (2017). The rise and fall of Marissa Mayer, from the once-beloved CEO of Yahoo to a $4.48 billion sale to Verizon. *Business Insider*, June 13, 2017. www.businessinsider.com/yahoo-marissa-mayer-rise-and-fall-2017-6. Accessed February 18, 2018.

Wigglesworth, Cindy. (2013). Empathy precedes compassion. *Huffington Post*, May 6, 2013. www.huffingtonpost.com/cindy-wigglesworth/empathy_b_2796460. html. Accessed March 10, 2018.

Wikipedia. (2018a). *DOCUMERICA*. https://en.wikipedia.org/wiki/DOCUMERICA. Accessed February 20, 2018.

Wikipedia. (2018b). *John H. White*. https://en.wikipedia.org/wiki/John_H._White_ (photojournalist). Accessed February 20, 2018.

Zak, P., Kurzban, R. and Matzner, W. (2005). Oxytocin is associated with human trustworthiness. *Hormones and Behavior*, 48 (5), 522–527. doi:10.1016/j.yhbeh. 2005.07.009. Accessed March 2, 2018.

Index